.., Neil not only teaches about God's power, but he also shows us what is the power of God and brings the presence of God into our midst...

   Yerry Tawalujan, Nat'l Christian leader, Indonesia

Body of Christ,

... If you want to break with tradition, get back to Biblical Christianity, have a Pentecost where the power of God comes down heals the sick, raises the dead, and equips the saints to take their inheritance as sons and daughters of God, and cover the land with house churches or groups planted mostly through signs and wonders, we recommended Neil and Dana...

   Gene Davis, Foreign Missions Foundation, Portland, Oregon, USA

Dear Friends,

This is to affirm that I have known Neil Gamble and his wife Dana for sometime. They are absolutely precious gifts of God. Both of them have gone to many places in India and conducted seminars on Saturation church planting. In these seminars, participants have not only learnt about church planting but have come back filled with the zeal of the Lord. Their teaching is biblically based and inspired by the Holy Spirit. In my opinion they are best teachers in the world on these subjects and I would recommend them wholeheartedly to anyone who is interested in seeing God's kingdom grow and multiply. They are also very good at removing the spots and wrinkles from the Bride, if you already have a good church planting program going.

  Shalom,

   Victor Choudhrie, National House Church Saturation Planting Leader, India

Neil and Dana Gamble have had a remarkable ministry in many countries bringing believers, including leaders, into a more intimate relationship with God. Their view of discipling is urgently needed, to correct the common error of teaching abstract doctrine without bringing disciples into life-changing, intimate relationship with God. They do not neglect biblical teaching but balance it with an intimacy with God that is born of the Holy Spirit.

   George Patterson

These Signs Shall Follow:

The Miraculous Memoirs of a

Foot-Dragging Disciple

Neil W. Gamble

Contents:

INTRODUCTION 5

FORWARD.. 12

I WAS TOLD I WAS REBELLIOUS 16

MY YOUTH, AND GOD WAITING FOR ME........... 23

WAITING 33

INTIMATE ENCOUNTERS WITH THE MIRACULOUS....... 42

PRISON AND A DIFFERENT PLAN......................... 46

WHAT YOU SAY IS WHAT YOU GET 56

THE FEAR FACTOR.. 59

LIVING WHILE WAITING....................................... 65

DISCIPLING: LIVING IN INTIMACY 81

HOLY SPIRIT SPEAKING AND THE RESURRECTION COMMANDS.. 86

CONTINUED LIVING WHILE WAITING................... 91

KOLKATA,..103

LIVING THE VISION...109

KNOWING WITHOUT READING. 116

TO KNOW—THE IMPORTANCE OF HEARING. 121

ADDING REALITY TO YOUR RELATIONSHIP 128

UNITY, COMMUNITY AND CHOICE....................................133

PRAYER, LISTENING AND BURN TESTIMONY 136

THE FOOLISHNESS OF LISTENING AND OBEYING.. 153

Introduction

We were in India training a group of Banjara men for ministry in late 2001. At the beginning of the forty-day training, I taught on prayer and Holy Spirit. I spoke from the story of blind Bartimaeus calling to Jesus (Mk. 10:46-52). With a great amount of passion I taught them to never let anyone tell them to quit calling on Jesus or to be quiet when they know that Jesus is the key to their plight. (I had become kind of a radical about Jesus and His promises being true over the years, so I push people pretty hard to find a personal audience with Jesus.)

After the training was over on the first day, one of the men who spoke English well, brought a friend, a middle-aged Banjara man to me for prayer. He never shared why he wanted prayer, but he had a serious limp, so I assumed that I should pray for that.

The next day, after our teaching time, again he came to me for prayer. This time he had no interpreter so he just came and stood before me, gesturing with his hands for me to pray over him. Every day at the end of the training, here came this little crippled man for prayer.

> Without sin, Christ and the Gospel have no meaning or mission. This is the devil's greatest feat of deception, to hide sin in our heart.

After about ten days of this, I started getting tired of his constantly coming to me for prayer. Besides, I had prayed every prayer I knew. I was tired of his pestering me. I emphatically began to tell him to go away and leave me alone, but it never worked because he didn't speak any English, and he brought no interpreter. He would just smile while I talked harshly to him and gestured wildly with my hands for him to leave, and then he would fold his hands, close his eyes and wait. I prayed some dispassionate prayers over him like, "Father, deal with his constant whining and begging"! I was kind of rude to him, but he never left me alone until I prayed each day.

At the end of forty days of training, graduation came. Dana, my wife, and I were leaving India for a while to travel to other countries and then home after they graduated. On this last day, as we were preparing to go to the airport and fly out, this man with the limp came to me one more time for prayer. Since I was leaving I had a little more compassion that day and prayed a nice prayer, short, but scriptural, and then I left.

When I came back to India two months later, one of the first things I was to do was to speak at a gathering of some 4000 Banjara Christian leaders. When I arrived, many of the leaders came and asked me, "Have you seen Jesus Feet?" To each of them, I would reply, "I do not know any Jesus Feet." They would all laugh and tell me, "Yes, you do." It got kind of frustrating as the day went on, but finally at the end of my speaking engagement, a small group of leaders and this man, whom I instantly knew, came. It was the man I had prayed

6

over for forty days. I did not notice the fact that he was not limping. He had brought an interpreter with him, and proceeded to hug me and through tears he said, "Thank you for taking the time to pray for me every day of our training! You did not know that before I came to the training, I had been to a doctor about my leg. They told me that I should have it amputated as it was infected, and it would kill me if I did not deal with it soon. I wanted to come to the training, and I knew if I had my leg cut off I would not be allowed to attend the school. So I told the doctors they would have to wait forty days. They told me I would be dead in forty days. That first day of our training, you taught us about prayer and calling on Jesus. I knew Jesus was the answer I needed! Each day you prayed for me, and although I was not healed, the infection never got worse. On the day of graduation you prayed for me just before they took me back to my home." (They put him on the handlebars of a bicycle and rode him home.) "I had scheduled the surgery, before we began the training, to have my leg taken off a few days after I got home from school. But, when I got home that last day and stepped down from the bicycle, I discovered I was healed! I turned and looked at the man who had pedaled me home and said,' My name is no longer Beshar (I do not remember his real name), it is Jesus Feet.' From that day until this I have done nothing but walk from village to village and tell them about my Jesus and how He healed me. He is now healing others through my story, and I have seen many come to Jesus through His love and the testimony He has given me."

At this point I was crying. How could I tell him what I had prayed over him, and had actually done when he asked me repeatedly for prayer over those forty days? I wept and cried out, "Oh, Father, forgive me for my callous behavior!"

In spite of my "prayers," which fortunately he did not understand, God healed this man. I repented, and will never forget the importunity of this man and the love Jesus has for us. What a blessing for Jesus to use this incident of forty days of "prayer" to change both our hearts. In the West, we tend to pray for 15 minutes to **see if God will move,** instead of praying **until** we see His promise come true or we die.

This story is just one event in my life of pursuing intimacy with God. It is one more teaching from the Master about the need to **take seriously** the work of Christ in us and to persevere in our quest to know Him. This and other incidents in my life have brought me to a place of being one of *God's men.*

This book is not meant to be a theological statement, nor even a great teaching. It is meant to be about the journey to intimacy (a close, personal, dynamic relationship) with God. When I use the word intimate or intimacy, it should be noted that what I am talking about is knowing someone in depth (a deep familiarity), knowing many different aspects of a person, or knowing how they would respond in different situations because of the many experiences you've shared with them.

Intimacy is both the ability and the choice to be close, loving, and vulnerable to the Father of all creation. It is the path to being sold out for God or being God's man or woman. The intimacy Father wants depends on trust, and might involve disclosing thoughts, feelings and emotions to each other in order to reach an understanding. Father wants to build a sense of community. It might involve sharing a duty or job without any spoken commentary. ("God's man" -- for the sake of words I am using "man" but let it be known that I am speaking of men and women becoming sold out and radical for Him and His kingdom, thus God's people in singular form, God's man).

The foundation of this work is scripture; the walk is spiritual, physical and mental. *These Signs Shall Follow* is a book that relates some of my experiences in my life-long journey toward a deep, close, personal, dynamic relationship with God. It is meant to give you hope that Scripture is true and God is real. My life scripture is found in Psalm 17 verse 15.... "As for me I will see Your face in righteousness and I shall be satisfied when I awake in Your likeness". (NKJV)

This book is a compiled group of stories about my walk with Jesus, Father and Holy Spirit. It is a journey of consecration and trial, hope and love. I hope that it will encourage you and move you to expect more in your relationship with Him. God loves you and He has a plan for each of our lives! He has a need of us becoming God's people! Most everything that you will read here took place in small groups, at work and play, or "outside" the "traditional church" setting. My wife and I were involved in traditional meetings, but not asked to participate much. We were considered to be a little too radical, too strong, or too out of control by most traditional pastors and leaders of Evangelical churches. I can think of only a few miracles actually happening in large church settings. Small group meetings are a part of Dana's and my life in Jesus, and we don't know how to exist without them. **Meetings** were designed for gathering together to pray, reach out, study, work out problems, exhort, edify and be family. Holding each other accountable and constantly meeting with others was and is normal Christianity for us. Our goal is to see the body of Christ being the body of Christ and not simply attending a Christian meeting once a week. I want to be *God's man* and I want others to find the same.

The testimonies I have written down in this book are to provoke you to look at your life and see where you truly are in your relationship with Father. I want you to discover that there is more you can experience with Father and to show you that you can have God show up in all aspects of living. You can be the person of God you desire to be!

A scriptural foundation is to be the basis of our relationship with God. Scripture is not to limit your relationship or give you a formula to work with. True intimacy with Father, Son and Holy Spirit is about ordinary people involved in a real friendship with God. In my relationship with Father, I have bought Him flowers. I have had coffee with Him. I have gone for walks with Him. I have visited heaven and sat with Him. I have gone to work with Him and asked Him a thousand questions about life, work problems, and my family. My personal journey is one filled with visions, dreams, and strange encounters at the least expected moments. There has been a bit of persecution along the way, needed to form character and strength for the battles that were to come.

The journey to becoming *God's man* is about touching people with His presence. You can't spend much time with God without touching people; that is what He is about...love. Love has to be shared to be real, and God's love looks a little different from the love that we share in the American church realm! What I am going to share is all about a hearing, emotional, close communion with the Lord on an everyday basis. It is about my life with Christ and my Father.

It is filled with a few strange encounters that I recognize may blow some theological thoughts and be hard to understand. I still can't explain some of them after years of thinking about them, but I have seen the effect of these events on my life as well as others, so will give Glory to God for all of them. Each chapter or part of this book should be read with this thought in mind, "God loves me and will work with me if I am willing to hear, trust and obey. My Father wants personal close fellowship with me". We are created to walk with Him as a father and close friend. I feel that my whole life, not just my "church life," is a testimony of being discipled by the Master into someone sold out for Him. It is intimacy without religion. God has discipled me into my present relationship with Him. When we disciple someone our discipleship should have the same goal; to bring someone else into an intimate relationship with Father, Son, and Holy Spirit; to the place of being "God's people". Discipleship should show and guide people into a dynamic relationship with God. I am still on the quest for a greater intimacy with Father, and Jesus is still my teacher. This journey to become one with Father is a continuing quest.

Forward

True humility is expressed in obedience to God and a lack of fear or need of man's approval.

I would like to share a small testimony that happened to me overseas recently. So many times, I am astounded when the Lord shows up and does something different and amazing while I am training others in discipleship or intimacy.

I was working with a small group of elders and pastors in Indonesia (late 2005). I had begun to teach discipleship/hearing God's voice.

In the midst of one of the sessions, the Lord kept bringing my eyes to this one young lady in the seminar. Each time I would glance her way, Holy Spirit would say, "Tell her, Your mother will be fine"! After several attempts at ignoring this prompting, I surrendered, stopped, and told her, "Your mother will be fine." She smiled and nodded and went back to taking notes. Again the Spirit moved me, "Tell her again." So I stopped and again I said, "Your mother will be fine!" About five minutes later, the Spirit prompted me once more, but this time I spoke with more authority and there seemed to be fire in the words, "Your mother will be fine!" Each word was spoken with sharpness and yet without condemnation. When I again looked her way she was gone. I thought I must have embarrassed her.

I did not realize what had happened. This meeting was the first one of a month's journey. While I was traveling through the country doing ministry, I would get calls periodically from this church and they were continually checking to see if I could squeeze in another meeting for them. It ended up that the last 2 days of ministry I had scheduled in this country were cancelled so I gave the time to this church.

At the end of the last meeting I did with them, the pastor came to me and told me there was one more thing I needed to do. He wanted me to meet some folks who were waiting at the back of the church. I was tired from so many days of travel and ministry with little sleep and non-stop teaching, so I asked, "Why?" He assured me that I wanted to meet these people. As we walked up to the people, I recognized one of the ladies because when we were doing worship, she had been dancing with the youth at the back of the church. She was not a young lady, so I had noticed and thought how wonderful it was to see her having such a good time. When I got close to where she was standing she came up and hugged me. Then, through an interpreter, she told me the rest of the story. (Her daughter had been the one I had told, "Your mother will be fine.")

Some years before she had been in an accident and it had messed up her back badly. Through the years, she had several operations and numerous medical treatments to correct the problem, but to no avail. There was one final operation that would make her better, but it cost so much that they would have to sell the family home to pay for the operation. The family had decided to do that for her, and was in the process of selling it when I had spoken to her daughter. At the _same time_ that I had spoken to her daughter; across town the Lord had healed her. Her daughter got home after leaving the training to find her mother who had not been able to walk -- Healed! They did not have to sell the house. Her mom was crying on my shirt as she told me the story.

Interestingly, years before, I had been speaking with the Lord about His healing the centurion's servant from across town and had told Him that I would look forward to the day when I would speak in one place and have someone healed in another. Almost 20 years later, after a few "minor" character adjustments and encounters with the enemy, I did not realize that saying, "Your mother will be fine" was actually saying, "Your mother is healed; go your way!" Somehow in the past 20 years of walking with Father, I had quit seeking the gift of healing and miracles for people to be healed through and simply began to seek Jesus and to know Him. Now, I am seeing the healings I longed for all those years.

I hope that in the midst of this writing, that somehow Holy Spirit imparts something special to you that will cause a passion for intimate fellowship with Father to spring up in your heart. You can be *God's person* in your family and community.

Many of the stories that you will encounter in this book are actually the answers to intense times of prayer I have gone through for years. At times I would cry for hours, repeating one sentence, "Father, save souls, send me!" At times I would spend days and even weeks pleading with the Lord, arguing with Him and reminding Him of His promises and commands. I would contend with Him for souls, plead for people to be healed, delivered, or set free at work, at home, as I fished or drove somewhere. It was and is in my heart 24/7. I was (and am) a radical, and most people would not pray with me for long during those times. At times, when praying for people, I would pray for Jesus to put their sins on my account and set them free. I would tell God that the Blood of Jesus was enough, have mercy. Not pleading for mercy, but telling Him what the scripture says. I was constantly asking Him not just to send me, but "anoint and send me,"

14

according to His promise to places no one else would go! My goal was not fame or fortune; I was working at the time, and supported our ministry with our own money. I was hungry to know Jesus and have His heart in me. I was and am still on a quest for it to be Christ who lives in me, and that I would be hidden in Him. I want it to be, "Not I that live, but Christ in me the hope of Glory" (Gal. 2:20).

Those prayers I prayed then, are so much a part of my life today; I continue to pray them and live to fulfill His desire in me, not my desire or vision. I want to experience Jn. 17:20-23; for it to be real that we should be "One" even as He and Father are "One." That path is a journey into selflessness and brokenness that brings joy and peace in the Holy Ghost. It costs nothing to be a believer, but it costs everything to be a disciple. Getting to Heaven is free; living for Jesus in this world could cost you your life. It will cost you the approval of man and a lot of your friends and family could be lost to you. As for me and my house, it is worth it and we will serve the Lord!

I Was Told I Was Rebellious

> Before the end, God the Father of all, will demand from his people a demonstration of the power, love, and character of Christ worthy of the day, hour, and time in which we live. (unknown author)

Man's quest for a meaningful expression of "Love" can be seen in all we do. Some search for it through sexual relationships, others through religious practices, and others through work, etc. We are constantly looking for a place or union that will provide an acknowledgement to us that we are needed, wanted, appreciated and valued. We constantly search for a place where we are physically, spiritually and emotionally fulfilled. It is hard to fathom the Love that God has for man or why he continues to be committed to it. After all we have done; adultery, idolatry, murder, hatred, violence, divorce, etc., why does God still love us and want us as a bride? Through all of the atrocities of time, God has remained faithful to His character and loved us in spite of ourselves. I think that we could spend a lot of time looking at God loving us, in spite of all we have done, and probably find out why the world does not like Christians. Our love is so shallow toward each other and strangely lacking the attributes of the Love God has for us. My son Phillip says that when you take God out of the word "love", or His presence out of our acts of love, you do not have love, because God is Love.

The world does not need the religion we have founded on the Bible, but they do need the God of the Bible. The Bible is about love and intimate fellowship with God, not simply what to do or not to do. The "do's and don'ts" are found in it as you read it from the "tree of

16

the knowledge of good and evil" perspective. Yet the Word is about a relationship with God; it is about Father's Love for His creation. It is a love story between God and man. In it you will find that God has such a great love for man, that He himself was willing to send His Word and have, "The Word become Flesh" (His son) to die for us, to restore and make the original relationship He desired possible. The Bible is a revelation of who He is and what it takes to have a close, personal, dynamic fellowship/relationship with Him.

There is a cost to being God's man and walking in a love relationship with God. There are some harsh incidents written in the Word because of our continued quest to do evil or our neglect to trust and pursue Him. You must give up anger, loneliness, fear, hatred, etc., and you must seek and receive faith, hope, love, confidence and peace to partake of the intimate fellowship He desires to have with us. Most of the Christian religion is founded on the principles of the Bible and conformity to religious activities that do not bring us to that dynamic relationship that Father desires. God is about relationship, and His desire is that there should be a freedom in Christ and a testimony of Jesus in our lives so the world might see what great love He has for all mankind. The testimony of Jesus is always miraculous, and it changes lives as it is lived in the midst of a dying world. God is not restrained by the Bible. It is the foundation of who He is and shows us the cost of life with Him and without Him. It shows the way to a relationship with Father. Jesus says, "You search the scriptures for in them you think you have eternal life but, these are they that testify of me!" (Jn. 5:39). What if you really believed that was true? How would that change the way you read the Bible?

When I keep in my mind that the written Word we have is to show us Jesus, who He is, what He likes, what He wants to see happen and

17

who I am in regard to God and love, I get a whole different revelation to a lot of scripture and find myself listening differently to the dialogue in my spirit with His Spirit.

I have sat in many congregations and found that most of them have room for only one man's vision, unfortunately. For many of my "church" years I had been told to sit down, shut up, and that eventually I would calm down! Because of my questions and my desire to do things so that I could be a part of what God is doing, I was told that I was rebellious. It was never in me to be rebellious. I was just hungry and wanted to be used by God and to know Him. I wanted to be needed. I was hungry to be a part of Christ and His Church, as a disciple, not a spectator. I have met countless others through the years that have told me they felt the same way. They were hungry to be emotionally fulfilled and to be needed and used, but were constantly told there was no place for their specific vision or ministry in the church they were attending. Their focus did not fit with the "vision of the house." Many of these believers quit trying to be used after rejection became the general response they received from leaders. They became "church hoppers" looking for a place to "fit." What a sad description to put on someone hungry to know and be needed by Jesus and Holy Spirit. Many are lost who were hungry to be a disciple of Christ. They have given up on being a part of what Jesus is doing because of rejection and pressure to conform to the traditions of man. Many of the others have become sitters instead of doers because they have had it pounded into their brain that they are meant to sit, in spite of being told to "go and do" by the Word.

When people continued to tell me I could not speak or teach or share through some subtle and some not so subtle rejections, I went back to scripture to see where I had missed it or what to do. All I could find was commands to be active and involved with Christ to "Go." Finally, I simply quit looking for a place to fit in or for leaders who would help me and I went out and began to do what scripture said. I could not get the approval of men no matter how hard I tried to conform, so I quit looking for it. I quit seeking it, (like Paul, I found that "Those who seemed to be something—(whatever they are), added nothing to me. Gal. 2:6."). I was through being told _not_ to do what scripture said I _must_ do "go" and get to "know" Him! As I went to the least, the lost, the prisoner, the widow and orphan, I found Jesus and I found a love relationship that still draws me. I decided to live what I read in scripture. I went outside the "traditional church" to the world and found that God was there seeking and saving the lost and destroying the works of the devil. I found places in prisons, parks and at work to do what I saw in scripture a normal Christian was supposed to do. Scripture and Jesus' commands became my life. I started to move forward into His presence. My walk with Him became my life! I found that as a "layman" I had a holy calling to live for Him. I am not trying to be negative about the traditional church, as we know it, because much of what I am today is because of my past church experience. I am saying that there needs to be radical change. We need to get back to the scripture and make our "church experience" more than one man's vision or walk. Pastors are some of the most misused people in the whole body. _They should stop doing the church's ministry and start training the church to do the ministry!_ (Eph. 4:11-13). Church is what it is today because we "the Church" allow it and at times demand it to be what it is. We need to read the Scriptures and conform our lives to them and stop conforming the scriptures to our lives.

We need to "hear" what the Spirit is saying to the church. Hearing is an essential aspect of life and relationships. Even the deaf can hear. They hear through the movements of others, through pictures, visions or movies, expressions, circumstance, writing, touch, rain, etc. Hearing has more to do with listening to all that is communicated, rather than listening to an actual voice speaking in our ears. Most Christians would do well to watch the deaf hear. It may teach us some of the ways God is speaking that we have come to ignore. We may find that God has been talking a lot more than we have heard. We may find a much bigger expression of His love and caring. We might see that He is more involved in our lives than we had previously accepted. We might find a way to hear what He is speaking. In most relationships, conversation is the foundation to the depth of the intimacy. The communication and communion that is shared between two parties dictates the depth of the relationship. If only speaking is involved in that communication, the relationship is generally shallow because a lot more is spoken than our simple words express.

Much of my learning about a relationship with God has come from life experiences and my relationship with my wife, Dana. It is she who has taught me many of the lessons on love that actually have shown me how to love my God and Father—to wait on Him and how to hear Him. It is a continuing journey.

I wonder what it would be like for the whole church to be in the place of understanding of all the different ways God speaks and moves in our life? What would the world be like if Christians actually expected to hear from God at work, at play, in the shopping mall, or in the car while traveling? What if the conversation was not about religious activities but life with Jesus? What would happen if the majority of Christians were expecting to hear from God in all situations

20

and God started to share truths about their work, friends or about the future? What if He showed Christians their friends' real fears and pains that are hidden behind the masks of clothes or laughter at work or at home? What if they heard from God about how to do their job? What if Christians started to pray from the place of hearing Holy Spirit instead of guessing what should be prayed over the situations in their family and friends lives? At times a flower speaks much louder than words, if you are listening.

There are so many experiences and challenges we encounter in life that make us who we are. Have you recognized that the position you see yourself in will affect what and how you hear? A son and a servant hear the same words quite differently. A servant is always worried about his performance because his job, life, and family de-pend on whether he pleases the master and obeys every command with diligence. His livelihood is based on his pleasing the Master. A son, on the other hand, never worries about his position with the Master because the master is his father. He does not worry about losing his place in the family or his bed to sleep in at night. He does not fear being imperfect in the performance of his duties. A servant does not live in the house with the master, but comes in and must be pleasing on each visit. He does not go to the Master when he wishes, but must be called by the master or summoned. A son gets up in the morning in the house of the master and thinks nothing of entering a room with him in it. They live together. There is a different bond be-tween them than the master has with the servant. Everything the master does is for his children to inherit. So then you see that if you consider yourself a son in your heart, you react differently than you would if you actually see yourself as a servant. A son does not even think about his position. He is who he is, and that is not to be attained or focused.

The position you see yourself or others in will affect what you hear or if you will listen to someone. If you do not place value on the person you are listening to, you will not truly hear what they say. You may hear the words they speak, but the words do not impact you as they mean nothing to you. If you have a high opinion of them you will attend to every word they speak.

Sometimes we don't want to hear as it causes comfort loss or requires too much of us. I want to know Father and walk with Him. I want to be called a friend of God. I want to be more than a man of God; I want to be God's man! Sold out for Jesus, nothing less will do. Hearing Father as a son and not a servant is important to my relationship with Him. I do serve Him, but I am not a servant; I am His son!

One of my life scriptures is; **Psalms 17:15 (NKJV).** [15] *As for me, I will see Your face in righteousness; I shall be satisfied when I awake in Your likeness.*

For me to receive the answer of many of my prayers and to be all that Jesus wants and needs me to be, has a lot to do with being able and willing to hear a little four letter word—WAIT! As children, we hate to hear our parents say, "Wait." This word takes trust because many times there is no explanation as to the purpose of "wait" to us. This word has a lot to do with intimate fellowship because it develops character and faith. Most of us hate it and have no patience for waiting. It is not a western cultural norm. Yet, waiting is something that God did for some time before He could release the Word, Jesus, into this world and our lives. Timing is everything and waiting is a part of learning about faith, hope and love.

My Youth, and God Waiting for me

> Victory is won the moment you open the door of your heart to believe.

As a young child I had time with the Lord, though none of my family really walked with Jesus. My mom tried to be religious two days a year - Easter and Christmas. My family was not Christ followers, but they were a good bunch to grow up with. Dad and Mom both had very high morals and lived with integrity. I found a relationship with Father and spent a lot of time talking with Him in the midst of this environment.

We raised sheep and then horses and cattle, so I was a shepherd of livestock from a young age. At the age of 11, I was left alone in the wilderness with a band of sheep at night and had to move them the next day to another place. My uncle was to come and stay with me and help me get the sheep where my dad was to meet us several miles away, but he never showed up and I ended up doing this drive alone. I am sure that is when I had one of my first encounters with God's provision and presence. I had talked with Him before as my unseen friend, but this time He became my support and actually helped me get the sheep to the destination without losing any . When you are alone with a band of sheep moving them at the age of 11, there is a bit of fear, and like we all do when we get into a tight place, I cried out in my desperation and fear to God and found Him faithful! He came to me and encouraged and guided me. Imagine -- an 11 year old with a band of sheep and no one to turn to for help, sheep going every which way and no one to guide me in how to not simply gather them, but move them to a new pasturing area. I can

23

remember the sobs and fear in me as I cried out, then peace and a knowing came of what to do first. I moved the sheep!

I know as I look back, this was the beginning of my education and life with Jesus. A lifelong conversation began during those days. As I lived and continued to work on dad's ranch, I ended up spending a lot of time by myself doing the work required to keep the ranch going. Dad drove truck to support the ranch and mom had a beauty parlor that she ran, so much of the chores and needs of the animals was left to me. Feeding the animals, moving them around, doctoring them and general ranch work occupied much of my time as a young man. So, in the midst of those times I talked with my friend, Jesus. I did not go to church, nor want anything to do with "Christians" as they were a bit religious and self-centered, I felt. They spent a lot of time on 'church activities', which I did not have time for. We had a pastor for a bus driver and several times he ran the bus into the ditch. Each time we, the kids, had to go get help as he would just sit there and pray. It did not leave a very good taste in my mouth about Christianity. During these early years with Jesus, He talked a lot to me about scripture, but I did not read the Bible, nor was I interested in one. By the age of 12 or so, I had such a strong relationship with the Lord that I was in a place of constant communication with Him. I did not realize until I was 30, and read the Bible for the first time, that He was teaching me scripture as He shared a place in my life. I thought that He was simply telling me stories and showing me things that were going to happen in the future because we were friends.

One day, during this period, I was sent out to our cold house (the place we stored our fruit, veggies and potatoes during the winter on the ranch) to get some fruit. As I was about to enter the cold house, Jesus spoke to me and asked me a question, "Will you stay?" I knew exactly what He was asking me even without any formal Bible education. He was asking if I would stay with Him to the end of time through a very hard troubling time and through quite a long journey. After He asked if I would stay He added, "Don't answer me now, take some time and think about it." In other words, He was giving me the option to choose this path He offered or make another choice. Once I answered this question and made a choice, there would be no going back. My decision and answer to Him would set a future before me that could lead me through some interesting and possible hard times and trainings. Yet He wanted *me* to choose. As I reflect back on that moment, I can still see myself standing with my hand on the door of the cold room listening to my Jesus ask me this profound question that would change my life. I was 12! I had not been in church except on Christmas or Easter. I had no training or instruction—except for my friendship with Him. He was standing next to me, and I could almost physically see Him. There was a deep sense of His presence. I am sure I was looking into His intense loving eyes and then turning, opening the door, I left Him standing there while I went to get the fruit for mom. It took me a few moments inside to ponder the words that He had spoken to me. I was at a loss as I thought, Who am I that He should ask me such a question? This is a question for grown-ups. That question is as fresh today as it was 46 years ago, like it was just a moment ago that He raised it.

It is like that with many of the experiences I have had with my Lord; they seem so fresh and new, yet years have passed since receiving them. Anyway, as I exited the cold room, I found that He was not standing waiting for me, but I knew He was near. I remember looking up toward the sky pondering how to put words to what was in my heart. "I don't know how to answer You. I have no idea of the future and what it includes other than what I feel You have told me. You said think about this, and I know this is important and that I should probably take more time, but I have only one way to answer your question. Somehow I know that you are my protector and more than a friend to me and in asking that question I know that You are trusting me, so I trust You, and because of that trust I will say this, 'Yes, I will stay with you' —to the end." As I said those words I knew that in that moment my life was changed. I felt immediately that something had just happened that I could not take back, not even in the first moments after I had said it. There was no turning back! I felt that the heavens had changed in the few moments that I had been in the cold room. I had goose bumps and shivered at the thought of what I had just done, and promptly put it out of my mind. Since that day, I have never been far from that commitment. It is there in my mind, lying there like a foundation stone constantly pulling me toward Him and into the future. No matter where I have gone and what I do I have never gotten far from the truth of that life- changing moment.

I was not a bad kid, but I certainly did my share of despicable deeds. I got in trouble at school and at home, but nothing really serious for the most part. I believed I was a great liar and was constantly telling some tall tale about what I had done or didn't do. I beat up a couple of kids and stole things constantly, yet Jesus was there the whole time, never leaving me, not approving, but never leaving.

When I was a little older, I was drinking and playing music in the bars at the age of 17, living life in the fast lane. I can now tell you that you cannot live in God's presence and have a continued conversation with the Lord and do these things. A wake-up call will come. When you continue to live outside the courtyard of God's plan He will come for a visit of a more profound type. Most of us do not recognize those visits; we tend to attribute them to coincidences or chance. Choices, (such a big part of our life), lead us to these visits that generally we do not recognize. God would speak to me, but I did not really believe that He knew everything, so I would do what I wanted in spite of what He told me. Looking back at some of my choices, I might change some of them; although I am very aware that _ALL_ of the incidents of my life make me who I am now, not just what I perceive are the good ones.

My buddy Charlie and I were going to take a week off before starting football practice and school between our junior and senior year. Mom even lent me her car for the trip. On the second day of our drunken excursion, I went to a swimming pool in Kettle Falls, Washington, where we were visiting friends. Showing off, I dove in, hit the bottom of the pool and broke my neck. The lifeguard got me out of the pool, but I was hurting bad. I still had movement, but was in such pain that I would black out every few moments. No ambulance was called and my friend drove me to the hospital. At the hospital after they had taken x-rays, I heard the doctors state that they were sure that I would not be kept there, so they did not want to do much of anything for me. They simply put me in a neck brace and left me in my bed. I had to get up and use the toilet and sit up to eat. I blacked out a couple of times, but it did not cause them to change anything. The cloth brace they had put on my neck did nothing.

Mom came the next day and they said that she could just move me in her car. We traveled about 250 miles with me lying in the back seat passing out periodically and being sick. When we arrived in Ellensburg and the doctor there was shown the x-rays from the first hospital, he asked my mom if the ambulance that had brought me to Ellensburg had left yet. He would not touch such a severe break, and

I needed to be shipped to a larger hospital in Yakima. She informed the Doc that I was lying in the back seat of her car. He was amazed and told mom not to move me at all! When we arrived in Yakima, they took me out of the car by strapping me to a board then lifting me off the seat and turning the board over and bringing me out of the car. They then strapped the board to a gurney. Immobilized, I was taken straight to x-ray again and after the x-rays were read I was put immediately into traction. The doctor told me as he was drilling holes in my head to attach the traction device, that I should not be alive. His amazement showed on his face and in his words. The seventh vertebra down on my neck was broken at both ends and the main piece was shoved forward out of alignment with the rest of my back. The broken pieces were lodged in the area my vertebra should have been. They hoped that the traction on my neck would allow the broken piece to slip back in line. I lay in that hospital for 30 days with increasing paralysis. I lost the feeling in my legs and had difficulty with my right arm.

At this point, the doctors decided to operate and fuse my neck before the paralysis got worse. The expectation was that I would remain a paralytic from the waist down, at the least, for the rest of my life. The announcement that they brought me was pretty disheartening for a cowboy and track runner (at that time I was the fastest kid in school and held several records for the sprints in track and field.) The day of the operation was to be the following Monday.

That Friday night in the late evening, as I lay in my dark room thinking of the future the doctors had shared with me, a Baptist clergyman from Seattle came in to my room. He was in Yakima visiting some of his flock that had been in an accident and were hospitalized there. As he came down the hall, the Lord directed him to enter my

28

room. He wanted to pray for me and tell me about Jesus. I knew so little about the Bible that I told him, "If you can show me Jesus in the Bible I will accept what you say." He pulled out the Gideon Bible from the drawer of my bedside table and proceeded to John, chapter one, and shared Jesus with me. All the years that I had talked to God and Jesus, I did not know that the Bible was about Him! For those of you who are traditional, you would say that I got "saved" that day. What happened was another step in my discipleship. Jesus, who had been my Friend for years, took another step into my life and became my Savior. In the darkened room a light appeared and grew in brightness until it flooded the whole place with brilliance. I said "Yes" to Jesus once again. As I was praying, it felt like a white-hot branding iron was being shoved up my spine from my tailbone to my head. I did not say anything about it to the Baptist minister who stood there praying, but I knew something was happening again in my life. When I had finished praying and the clergyman had left, I lay and talked with my Friend and now Savior, Jesus. I did not know that I was healed. I told Jesus that if He let me walk out of the hospital the way I had been before I came in that I would read His Word from cover to cover. God has such a great memory. Years later I would be reminded of that moment. In the midst of that long night, Jesus came and spoke to me about the future and called me to follow Him and live for Him. It was my call to be a "man of God." The calling scared me because I was sure that if I said yes to what He was asking that He would send me to Africa and I was a cowboy raised with a lot of bigotry around me. I did not answer Him that night. In fact, it took almost 14 years before I would answer His call and surrender. The question was there all the time, but I learned to ignore its pestering presence. Only one problem, which I did not know, where can one go to avoid God and His voice?

The next morning at 5:30 A.M., as usual, they came and x-rayed my neck to see if there was any change. From the time of the x-ray till about 9:00 am there was a nurse in my room. I thought they were just being nice. I did not realize that I had bent my legs or that I had put the milk that came with breakfast onto my chest with my right hand. I did not realize that I was moving my lower body constantly.

At nine, the doctors who were going to operate on me on Monday, came into my room dressed in golf clothes (evidently they had been out playing when they got called to the hospital). They brought in an x-ray viewer and two x-rays. One of the doctors came to my bedside and began removing the traction device from my head and taking out the screws that held it in place while the other was explaining what was going on. Pointing to one x-ray, he noted the broken vertebra pushed out the front of my neck and the broken pieces. He then went to the other x-ray which was of a perfect spine and I heard him say, "The first x-ray is of your neck yesterday and this one is your neck today."

I had no idea what was going on. The doctor next to my bed unhooked all the cables and said quietly, "Son, you will have to look to a power higher than we are for what has happened here because your neck is healed and you are taking up space that someone who is sick could use!" On the day that they were to operate on my neck, I left the hospital walking.

Needless to say, although Jesus had become my Savior, I very soon forgot about my promise to read His Word from cover to cover if I was healed, and I hid from the calling that He had brought with His healing. I went back to drinking, riding horses, playing music in the bars and being the master of my own life. There was one difference: whenever I got to drinking too much or doing drugs late at night, I would begin to tell people about Jesus and how He had healed me, how He was the answer to whatever they needed. After a few months, whenever I had been partying for a few hours my "friends" would all start abandoning my presence because they knew that the inevitable time of preaching about Jesus was coming. I could not tell my folks anything about my experience because they were pretty adamant that Christians were losers and did not want to hear about God. He was the favorite curse word around the house. I told everyone else what had happened.. for the next thirteen or so years. (Usually my guard only came down enough to give in to His presence when I was drunk or stoned.)

Through all those years, Jesus was faithful to teach and train me for what I would need to know to be doing the ministry now, that I had not surrendered to do then. I would be working, playing or doing whatever- it did not really matter. In the midst of anything I was doing, Jesus would be talking to me and showing me how to do something, or simply would be there as a friend. I was in several car accidents and close calls at work, but would walk away unscathed. Once, when I was breaking a young horse while I was home alone, I decided I needed to ride this horse since I was bored. This was a really stupid idea because if anything went wrong there was no one to help me. Nonetheless, I caught and saddled the horse and was riding him. I decided to go out in the sagebrush with this green broke, unstable young horse. He did pretty well for a while, and I kind of relaxed. At that point, a rabbit jumped out and the horse leapt sidewise violently. I was thrown, and my foot was hung up in the stirrup. The young brown colt did not bolt immediately, but was standing looking back at me on the ground. It was getting nervous and I knew it would bolt at any time. I reached and got my pocketknife, then slowly, as I talked calmly to this young horse, I raised myself to the point that I could stick the knife into the stirrup leather and cut it so my foot would come loose. As I reached with my knife to cut the stirrup, the horse jumped and began to run. Somehow I managed to cut the leather and it gave way in the first lunge.

I lay on the ground and looked up and knew I had just missed death. It is amazing how clearly God can get your attention in such moments. I thanked Him, picked up my stirrup and headed for the corral and a beer. What was the chance of that horse not running off instantly? What caused him to wait for the moment it took for me to get my knife out and be able to cut the leather of the stirrup? What caused the rabbit to leap out? Oh, there are so many things that I wonder about. God had not forgotten my "Yes" at the age of twelve, nor the one at seventeen, nor my unwillingness to surrender my life to Him as Lord. I thought that I was making all my decisions and making my own way, but I did not know the scripture that says, "The steps of a righteous man are guided by the Lord." Men might not have called me righteous, but God did. That is what His Word says, "Jesus is my righteousness!" If any Christians had known that I knew the Lord during those times they would have called me a backslider or rebellious, but I was simply walking with my Friend and Savior Jesus the best way I knew how.

Waiting ...

> Pentecost did not teach the disciples anything; it <u>made</u> them the incarnation of what they preached.

At the age of 30, in the beginning of my walk with Jesus as Lord and not just Savior and Friend, the word "wait" became a dirty word to me, as I did not understand the word nor the significance of it in relationships.

I should have known more about the word, after all those years of talking with Jesus, but I have little patience to sit and so, **wait** was not a part of my vocabulary. It is neither relaxing nor rewarding to me.

When I first started walking in the church, I was always coming up against that word—wait! "Wait until you have more training, wait, this is not the time, wait, you don't have the authority to do that." In my experience the word wait was right next to the word "sit down" and those words told me that I had no significance in the body of Christ.

When I began to read the Word, (at the age of 30), I was confident that it was God's book because it contained incidents that He had shared with me before I read it. I knew about healing, deliverance and guidance by Holy Spirit long before I read that this was His will for people. He would talk to me about hate and unforgiveness and how they destroy people's lives. He talked to me about the last days before His return and what it would be like. Looking back, after reading the Word now, some of the things He shared with me as a young kid were astounding.

We went through a lot together, and He was always faithful even though I was not. So many times He pulled me from near disaster and death before I had surrendered to Him as Lord. He was always there talking to me, serving me, helping me even when I was cussing or doing things totally wrong, like selling drugs. I had several close calls with death: two car wrecks, nearly shooting myself with a shotgun crawling through a fence, etc. I regret a lot of those years because at the age of 17 He called me to follow Him when He healed me. I wish I had a good excuse for not following Him as Lord during that time, but I do not. I just did not want to be a "minister" nor did I want to obey Him. The Christians I knew looked like hypocrites, (unlike my own walk which was so good and straight—not!) The church does not have a monopoly on hypocrisy. Life is filled with those not trying to be hypocrites who walk in hypocrisy.

At the age of 30, much of life as I knew it and had lived it, was destroyed. I lost all I had: a business, some land, even my reputation. After all this time of talking to Jesus or about Jesus to my drug addict friends, I had started to read the Word. I found stories and facts that Jesus had taught me long before I had ever picked up a Bible to read it. I began to go to church. My wife grudgingly went with me and found Jesus after a time.

I had made Father a promise to read His word from cover to cover at the age of seventeen, thirteen years before while lying in a bed with the future of a paralytic. I had forgotten that promise, conveniently, until the   Lord reminded me. As I was reading the last few verses in the book of Revelation in our home in Pasco, Washington, my four-year-old son Jon who was playing on the floor with a truck, looked up at me and began to speak, "Dad, I hear bells ringing. Dad! I hear bells ringing!" (There were no bells ringing in the physical).

"Dad, did you know that God is Jesus and Jesus is God?" He then went back to playing with his truck on the floor. The phone rang, and in one ear a man was offering me a job in Nampa, Idaho, and in the other the Father was speaking. "Son, this is my will for you. Son, if you turn from me one more time, I AM NOT FOLLOWING!" He proceeded to show me how many times He had saved me or kept me from destruction through the years. I knew that my time running from Father was over! That was the day that Jesus became Lord of all. It is amazing how we can know the voice of God, and still not consider all He does to bring us to true freedom and life.

Father moved us away from my old friends and we started a new life in Idaho. We began to attend a denominational church and "learn about religion" and a different Jesus than I had known up to this point in my life.

Father has a way of bringing into your life choices that He wants you to make but will not simply thrust them upon you. He works with our will and our choices to bring us to Him and to real freedom. God's predestined plan for us does not make us robots. God works with us as we write the future with our choices. His overall plan will come to pass, but it is in working with us that He accomplishes His desires in our lives and on earth. We do have a choice. "Choose this day whom you will serve." (Joshua 24:15)

In my zeal I started to pray a lot while continually devouring the Word. I wanted more of Jesus. I was so hungry and felt that there had to be something more because I felt not quite full. I could not witness like I wanted, there was still some kind of fear in me that held me back. What a rush those days were! I would rant and rave about what I was learning, but had no ability to convince people that what I was sharing was true.

As I was praying for **more** I was also working as an electrician on a corporate farm. I would listen to Christian music on the radio every day, and one day as I was doing my work, I heard, "tonight at such and such Junior High School." I heard nothing else because of the noise around me. Several times I would hear this same announcement and was perplexed at not hearing all of it. I did not hear who, when, or what, simply the location. As the day wore on it became frustrating to hear only the location and "tonight." By five-thirty that night I was so filled with a need to go to this *whatever* that when I got home I simply came in, showered, changed clothes and told Dana that I had to go to this meeting, and I did not even know what it was about.

At that time we were going to a church that did not believe in the "baptism of the Spirit" and had taught us that it was of the devil and to be avoided. So we avoided anything to do with "the experience." I went to the location where the meeting was to be held, arriving at about six or so, and sat in my car, waiting to see what would happen. In a while, an older couple showed up and was unloading some boxes from their car. As I was just sitting there, I asked if I could help them carry their boxes into the school. As I did this for them and helped them set up the book table at the entrance to the school auditorium, it never occurred to me that they were whom I was coming to hear.

I did not see the cover of their books or read the pamphlets they laid out. It had to be God because the speakers were Charles and Frances Hunter whose ministry is predominately focused on getting people filled or baptized with Holy Spirit. They even asked me to watch the table for them as they wanted to go and get a cup of coffee before the meeting. I was selling their books and collecting money for a couple that I had never met. Crazy! When they came back, I went into the auditorium and sat at least 14 rows behind the last row of people in the place. As it filled up I would move further back. I had no idea of why God had me there and what would happen, but I certainly didn't want to get too close.

As Charles Hunter came out and began to share about Holy Spirit, he would speak in tongues every once in a while and shared about fifteen minutes or so. I thought to myself, "This is why you brought me here Lord; to see how the devil works!" I was thrilled.

As I thought that, Charles looked up at me and began to speak to me. Now, remember I am fourteen rows behind the closest person, so there is no mistaking whom he is speaking to and he is waiting for me to answer his question. "Do you want to receive more of God?" I nodded in agony at being singled out by this man I thought was deceived by the devil. He then read Lu. 11:13, "How much more will the Father give the Holy Spirit to those who ask!" and sent me another question, "Can you agree with that scripture, son?" Again I nodded, and he proceeded to call all who wanted to receive more from God to come forward for prayer. I did not move, but slid a little lower in my seat as I watched this spectacle unfolding before me. I was mystified by the amount of people in the room who were being deceived by the enemy. To my dismay, Charles looked up at me once more, and with an authority I did not understand, he spoke to me. "If you want more of God come on down here," and with a gesture of his hand summoned me to come. I felt a different hand grab me by the back of the shirt and lift me from my chair and thrust me into the aisle. I stumbled and looked around to see who had shoved me into this place. No one was there, and I turned to see every eye on me waiting for me to come to the front. I strolled down the aisle and stopped about five feet behind the last of the crowd at the front of the theater-type auditorium.

Charles once more looked at me and asked if I would pray for all the people there, including myself, to receive all that God had for them. "Can you do that, son?" I nodded in agreement and he went on, "Can you pray that you would all receive Holy Spirit?" I did not need to affirm that, evidently, because he went on and told me to pray that God would baptize, fill, and anoint each of us with Holy Spirit and give us all that we could get while on earth from the Lord. He then simply stood there and waited for me to pray. I did not move and soon many of the people were turning to look at me waiting for my prayer. I started to pray, and Charles stopped me and told me to lift my arms and pray loudly for all to hear. I was a bit miffed but continued with arms raised to the sky. As I finished the prayer, I no-ticed that many around me started to cry and speak in tongues as the Spirit gave them utterance. To my dismay, I found tears on my own cheeks and noticed --- I was praying in tongues!

Instantly, I was mad, and rushed from the room, ran to my car and headed home. I was furious! God had deceived me and let the devil take control of my lips. I had trusted Him, and now I was talking in *tongues.* I told Him in no uncertain terms that I was truly upset and was going home and getting my Bible and that He better show me the scriptural truth about what had happened to me, or we were through. If I could not trust Him, and He let me be deceived, then we were done! When I got to the house and walked in my wife met me and asked instantly, "What happened to you?" I quickly retorted, "Nothing," and then added, "I am going into my study, don't wait up for me." With that I closed the door to my study, and God and I had a long talk through scripture. He guided me to scriptures I had never seen or knew of, and at the end of a long four hours, I left my studies, and went to bed saying, "Ok, I receive what you have given, Lord, and am sorry for not trusting you. Thanks for showing me the truth." I was "baptized" in the Spirit and another step in my education began!

I had to drive to California City, California, the next day (a 14 hour drive) and stay for two weeks, doing some work on some irrigation equipment my boss had developed. As I got into my truck to drive away, I began to sing with the radio, and instead found myself speaking in tongues. Hours later, I had to stop for gas in Nevada somewhere, and as I got out of the car to go in and pay for my fuel, I found that I could not speak in English. When the attendant asked me how much I had put in, I started to respond, but the only thing that would come out was mutterings and groans! It was hilarious! Every time I tried to tell her something, all that would come out was tongues! After a bit, she sent another guy out to the pumps to get the information she needed.

In the next two weeks I found the most amazing revelations of God's love as I studied His Word and prayed.

We saw quite a few miracles during these times. They started to show up after my Holy Spirit encounter. I would share or pray anywhere, at any time. I was loaded with zeal and hunger to know Him. The church was not ready for me. I am not sure my family was ready for me. They did not know how to handle my need to walk with Jesus in Spirit and Power. In my everyday life and at work I saw quite a few come to the Lord. I would immediately begin discipling them and getting them to go with me to pray for others and go after more souls. We became connected with some other radicals our own age, and everywhere we went, Jesus happened. What a time we had! We had some great ministry times, in spite of the fact that the church did not believe we had the experience or training to walk like this.

One time I was at work for an irrigation development company and needed to talk with my boss. I went to this irrigation water pumping station to see him. When I got there, he and another young man were working on a 100-horse motor/pump operating on 460 volts. There were several water pumps, and one of the control panels for these pumps was open. I assumed that it was the one for the pump they were working on. There were a couple of inches of water on the concrete. As I was standing in this water looking into the panel, I noticed a loose connection. (I was an electrician). I went to my car and got an Allen wrench (which is 3/8" x 6" of solid steel) to tighten this connection. I proceeded to tighten not only that connection, but also several others in the panel while I was standing in this water waiting for my boss to finish what he was doing so I could talk to him. (He was a Mormon and studying to be a bishop at the time.) As they finished working on the pump, he got up, came to the panel next to the one I was working on, and switched it on. As he did this, we both realized that I had been working on a different panel than the one that was turned off. The panel I was working on was **live**! I looked at him, then at the panel he turned on, then at the Allen wrench in my hands, and then at the panel I had been working on. Slowly I turned and went to my car and put the Allen wrench back, then walked out into the field next to the pumps, where I fell to my knees and worshiped God for a few minutes. After a bit of time, I got up and went back to my boss, who says, "I know that what happened just now was a miracle of God. You should be dead! There is one thing I don't understand though; you go to the wrong church!" What a witness of Jesus' grace and love!

(You need to understand that electricity rated at 480 volts is very dangerous and deadly. It kills, and what I had done was put a very large piece of solid metal into a live 480 volt panel that runs a very large pump. The fuses are not going to blow until you are dead, if you do what I did. By standing in water and leaning against the metal panel I was the perfect path for electrical current to pass through me, right down one arm, through my heart, and out the shoulder in contact with the metal panel or out through my feet immersed in the 2 inches of water).

You will find another story later where this same Mormon boss said almost the same thing after another miracle happened to me while working for him. God loved that man so much, he allowed the incidents and my not being shocked or killed just for him. The miracles really bothered him, and I got the opportunity to share about my Christ with him, and quite a few other Mormons, as a result.

I have had many miracles happen like this one in my life as I pray daily, "Send me, whatever it costs. Use me, Lord. I want to know you". I would not pick these kinds of incidents, but they do seem to happen in my walk.

Christianity is divine power in action. It is the Holy Spirit making the Word of God happen. The Gospel of Christ is alive. "With God, all things are possible." (Mk 10:27)

The greatness of Christ's demand upon us shows how confident He is in the promises He has put within us. "I can do all things through Christ." (Phil.4:13)

Through those years of my Christian walk, I was healed of third degree burns, saved from several very deadly situations with machinery, and saw several really wonderful healings in others, which will come up later. I had a lot of prophecies spoken over me about having the double anointing of Elisha and I was told to always wear the mantle of love and not to take it off. In spite of all the prophecies and miracles we saw during those days, people stayed away from the meetings I was involved with by the thousands.

Some friends of ours talked me into beginning to do prison ministry, and the Lord moved as I went. During this period I gave testimony at Full Gospel Businessmen conventions, Gideon's meetings, cowboy camp meetings, and retreats around the Northwest.

Somewhere in this early "church time," the Lord spoke something profound to me through a good friend that we ministered a lot with. We were sitting in my truck on a hill overlooking a town we were ministering in when the Lord spoke to my friend. He told him that he was doing ministry reasonably well and could lead others into His presence but He said, "You do not know Me!" I knew at once that the Lord was speaking to me also, because since I had started to go to "church," people had talked me out of much of my intimate fellowship with Him. For several years, people had told me that God does not talk to us like what was happening in my life anymore. They would say that "we have His Word now, and that is how He talks; through His written Word." I knew that as my friend was speaking, God was calling me back to a pursuit of His presence again. There is more to a relationship with God than reading the written Word. It is a part of our foundation, but there is so much more. My walk was a little too radical for most and it bothered people when I kept saying, "God said," or "the Lord showed me." I could not separate my walk with the Lord from everyday life and I did not want to. I encountered God more at work than anywhere and still encounter him more in simply living than I did in most church meetings. God has always shown me how to fix machinery, how to do my work more effectively, and He has always talked to me and helped me with anything I was doing. He also keeps telling or showing me things about other people's lives as I walk out my life doing work or being with them in restaurants or simply enjoying life.

Here is one example of Holy Spirit helping me at work and showing people God is alive. One of my bosses told one of his rich friends who owned a potato processing plant that I could fix anything. A machine at this other man's plant broke down shortly after his encounter with my boss, and his men could not seem to find the problem. He called my boss and asked if I was available. (Now think about this, my boss tells his friend about me and immediately this event happens—what are the chances of that?) I was close by, so my boss radioed me and sent me to this plant. When I walked in the door, I had no knowledge of any of these machines or of the plant. Several maintenance people met me at the door and showed me the machine that was not working. My eyes were drawn to a small box on the wall across from the malfunctioning machine. The maintenance leader saw me looking at this box, reprimanded me, and told me that I was here to fix the machine that was broken and not to be staring at some box on the wall. I sent this man to get me some blueprints of the machine and the others to get some tools and meters. When they left, I went to the box on the wall because I could not get away from the thought that this was where the problem was. Upon opening the box, I found some loose wires and fixed a connection in the box. As I was closing this box, the lead man came back with the prints, and one of the others came with some tools. I asked them to start the machine, or try to, so I could see what was happening. The lead man pushed the little green button and it ran. He asked me what I had done. I explained to him that the box in the wall that "had nothing to do with the machine" had a loose wire connection, and I had repaired it. They found that it was a connection box not shown on the prints. God had shown me that box and put it in my head that the problem was there. That machine was running in five minutes—isn't God good? They had been working on it for hours. Only God could have shown me that. There were many more incidents like this one through the years, and they continue to happen today. My Father loves to show Himself strong on behalf of those who love Him and are willing to listen and trust Him. He places us in jobs to make His presence known and His wonders shown to the world. Each man's vocation is a Holy Calling, not simply work. A full-time minister is someone who lives 24/7 for Jesus and does his work as a Holy Calling, not someone who ministers two or three times a week in a church setting. It is in life that intimate fellowship with Father is experienced while doing what needs to be done. God says that He is always with us so I talk and listen to Him. I wait on Him. He is my constant companion. Miracles happen when we are listening and obeying. Whether you are a machinist, driver, cowboy, housewife, electrician or whoever, if you are willing to ask the Lord to help you in life, whatever you do can turn into a miracle if we are willing to "wait on the Lord" and hear after having asked Him for help. A man of God is not simply one whose name is known in heaven, but he is also known in hell as God's man. If you look for Father in all your living, you will find Him and you will find instances where He will talk to you about more than your job or duties. He will show you needs in others and their pains so you can pray for them and encourage them. The more you include Him, the more you know of Him. The making of God's man requires us to fill our time with His presence, to practice including Him at every turn. If you do this, soon you will not start to do anything without asking Him for help or talking to Him first. In the small things, we find our intimacies with Him and they blossom into bigger things. The habits of living with Him daily change our future and that of those we encounter. Thus, we become God's man or woman!

Prison and a Different Plan.

> Faith is the divinely given certainty that the impossible will happen.

It was not uncommon for us to see miracles while ministering with the Evans in Idaho during the early 80s. One such miracle happened while I was going with them to do ministry in the Idaho state correctional facility.

We arrived to find the captain of the guards and the chaplain waiting for us. They told us there were a couple of groups of prisoners signed up for chapel that day who only wanted to fight with each other in the service.   (Chapel is one of the few places where different dorms can come together. The rest of the time, men in the different houses or buildings, are kept separate). The captain explained that he could not do anything to these prisoners as they had done nothing against the rules as of yet, but the guards felt that in the chapel service there would be a fight. One group was skinheads (racists) and the other was a Hispanic gang. He explained we were in a certain amount of danger, but that he wanted us to do the service so they could deal with the leaders of these groups.

The guards had things pretty well laid out and showed us what to do when the violence erupted. They had even rearranged the chapel so there would be a comparatively safe place for us to move to when the violence broke out. Of course I said "Let's do it." I always like a challenge and a little excitement. Carrie, the lady with us, stayed out, returning to the car, and the two of us guys went in.

We got into the chapel and when the inmates began to arrive they immediately started casting signs (making gestures with their hands) to one another and putting each other down verbally. This was a prelude to building up their bravado to engage in the fight that was planned. They taunted each other with racial slurs and curse words. My friend Lyle tried to do some worship with song and his guitar, but was told to shut up by the prisoners. So I stood up and began to share the Word with them. They told me in no uncertain terms, with a bit of profanity, that I should shut up also because they had other plans; theirs was a plan for war, and they were not interested in any religious programs. With several more curse words, they went back to baiting each other to begin the war and ignored me standing there in front of them with my Bible in hand.

Something rose up in me that I can never explain. It happens occasionally still. Sometimes I get very zealous about my Lord and this intense feeling rises up in me, as it did that day. I got right in the face of the short, close cut, blonde-haired, blue eyed, tattooed leader of the skinheads face and explained to him that this was a religious service and not a war zone. He, not so eloquently, told me to sit down before he did something violent to me.

Full of a boldness I could not explain, (God knows that I have a little of the cowboy nature in me, and He added some Holy Ghost boldness I am sure) I leaned forward and replied, "You came here with a plan to riot, but God has a different plan. Why don't you let me pray for you?" The skinhead leader exclaimed, "Go f--- yourself, preacher!" I spoke a little calmer and yet with a clarity that you could feel over the whole room of the chapel, "What...you chicken?"

Instantly it got intensely quiet. I had stepped into their turf. If this skinhead leader did not let me pray for him, the skinheads would have already lost the turf war because he backed down to *my* challenge. There was a lot of mocking from the Hispanic gang members in the room. The skinhead leader I had confronted relented, at the threat of being labeled a chicken, and with much chagrin I was told to go ahead and pray, "But make it quick and then get the *#_$** out of the road." I had him stand up, and as my hand rose to touch his head, Holy Spirit showed up. "In the Name of Jesus" is as far as I got in my prayer before he hit the floor. He was out! The Holy Spirit was all over him! He was shaking and mumbling, lying on the floor. It was evident that he was having a "special" God experience. There could be no other answer. I had never seen anything like it! I had heard of things like this but I had never experienced anything that remotely touched the power in that room. The guards started to come in, but my friend the musician hiding in the safe place, waved them out and explained quietly that God had laid this man out, not me. I have to say here -- **I was pumped**! From that point on I had the floor, except where the skinhead leader was laying. I was stepping over him, walking back and forth, and gave them the Truth of the Gospel. I preached a Gospel of power that God had already demonstrated. I don't remember what I said, but at the end there were seven or eight skinheads and Hispanics, who had come to fight each other, standing together, crying and accepting Jesus and being prayed for. Everyone knew that God had shown up and all of those present who weren't touched by Holy Spirit were really eager to leave when the gate was called, (that is when the prisoners are told to move back to their cells over the PA system), because what had transpired in that room was way out there...and extremely powerful!

The leader of the skinheads was still out on the floor while all that was going on. He was praying in tongues, weeping and shaking at times. The guards came in and were peeved because they did not get to deal with the two gangs. Instead, there was this young man on the floor, mumbling, groaning and making strange sounds while inmates and other gang members were leaving in tears. They told us to get him up or they would have to throw him in the hole (solitary). Their attitude cracked me up, they were not happy that Holy Spirit had shown up. My friend and I got this "has been" skinhead leader between us with his arms over our shoulders and walked him down the hall. He was so drunk in the Spirit that he had no idea what had happened and could hardly walk without support. This young skinhead fell down to the floor a very bad man and came back up saved, delivered, filled with Holy Spirit and totally changed. Now that will blow your theology! It did mine. No sinner's prayer, no repenting, no prayer time, no preaching—just Holy Ghost. I wonder if that is similar to what happened to Paul?

That was the last time I was at the prison in Idaho, as we moved shortly after this meeting. I didn't hear the rest of the story and what happened until about 12-13 years later. We had moved several times through two states since the initial incident.

Now about 12-13 years later we were in Glide, Oregon, attending an Assembly of God fellowship. One of the faithful of this AG church, Gordon, and the pastor wanted me to go fishing on the ocean with them. They had some people they wanted me to witness to and were adamant that I go. I get deathly sick on the ocean and therefore I do not do the ocean! I told them they didn't need me, they could do this ministry themselves. For goodness sake, they were an elder and a pastor and should have the experience to do just that. Finally, they

49

asked me to pray and ask God if I should go, and if God told me not to go, then they would leave me alone. I am not sure that God actually spoke to me, but I began to feel guilty for not being willing to go and help them win these people to the Lord. So, I accepted their invitation and hoped that God had changed me physically so I would not be sick. It turned out that I was not so blessed.

I need to inject here that I was not in a good place at the moment this event happened, I was a little depressed at what was not happening in my life. I had been wondering about some of my memories and asking myself if they really had happened and this skinhead event in prison was one of them.

As I had expected, after about thirty minutes on the ocean I was sick, gut wrenching sick! The people were being witnessed to all right, but not about Jesus. Instead, I showed them how sick a man with a tendency to motion sickness can get on the ocean. After about four to five hours of me continually retching, the first mate went to the captain and they decided that because I was so sick, they must quit early. The others had caught a lot of fish, so most were not too disappointed to go in after only half a day of fishing.

When we got to land, I was the first one off. I went up to a pole on solid ground and immediately leaned against it with my eyes closed. An older dockhand came to clean the fish the others had caught; I was busy holding that pole up, making sure it did not move! A young man came up on a bicycle and stopped next to the pole I was holding up. As I opened my eyes and looked at him, the thought came that he was running from the Lord, so I asked him, "Why did you walk away from the Lord"? "I have not walked away from Him," came back the retort. I was not in a very good humor at this point so I said, "Don't waste my time; Father said you were not walking with

Him, He misses you since you have walked away from Him." This young man had a baseball cap on so I could not see his face as it was below me, but he hesitatingly conceded and started to tell this story... "About 12 years ago I was in prison in Idaho and I was a leader of a racist group there. One day we were going to have a fight with a Hispanic gang in the chapel and this radical preacher named Neil Gamble came in and" ... he described the story of what I have already told! At this point I was in shock, and overwhelmed at his statements. I was still sick to my stomach, but that was changing fast at his recollection of the incident. Remember the people on the boat that the pastor and other faithful fellow wanted me to witness to? They are suddenly listening because they know my name is Neil Gamble. This young man on the bicycle proceeded to share how soon, after I left the prison (after the "war" meeting in which he was transformed), there was a revival in the prison. Many got saved be- cause of what the Lord had done in his life and the other gang mem- bers who had gotten saved. He became a Christian leader, and saw God move miraculously through things he said and did. The prison had a move of God sweep through it. (Later, I was doing prison min- istry at this prison with Bill Glass Ministries and the chaplain recog- nized me. He told me about the revival and what had happened after our last meeting that confirmed this man's story). They had seen real revival for a couple of years through this young racist who had be- come a Christian.

The young man continued to explain that about a year or so after his Christ encounter, he was suddenly called back to the county he was convicted in with no explanation as to why. In the county jail, while he was waiting to go to court, he led many of the prisoners and guards to the Lord. When he got to court the judge asked him if he knew why he was there, and of course he answered, "No." The judge asked the prosecutor and the defense counsel; no one knew why they were there. With a single stroke of his gavel, the judge commuted this young man's sentence! No explanation or reasons were given. The judge died a few weeks later, but never explained why he had commuted this young man's very long and serious sentence. It was investigated by *60 Minutes I was told,* and they never did get to the bottom of the mystery. The young man continued with his story, and said that after he was released from prison he became a youth leader in a church and gave his testimony at a lot of Christian meetings.

One day a lady from his past came and he stumbled back into drugs and other bad behavior patterns. The years passed and his story comes to the end as he said, "About two years ago I started to pray that this preacher, Neil Gamble, would come back into my life. I knew he could help me get back to God again. I have really wanted to get straight with the Lord, but I need help and I knew if God would just bring this radical preacher back into my life, I could make it." Everyone had been listening to this young man speak and had gathered close around us to listen to his story. I leaned down toward him and gently asked him his name with my hand outstretched to shake his. He responded with "Tom" and I replied, "My name is Neil Gamble," as tears were forming in my eyes. He fell down, grabbed my knees and wept. He cried and cried while he hugged me and was filled with such joy. The whole group went to lunch and sat and listened as we talked and I prayed for him. I visited him again a few weeks later, but do not know what is going on in his life now. God did answer His prayer, though. Intimate fellowship with the Lord is, most times, a spontaneous interaction with Life, while trusting and listening to Him.

The owner of the boat we had been out fishing on that morning, or for some of us chumming on, came to me after we had this encounter, and told me that her husband and she had been praying for years for something like this to happen with their fishing business. One of the men that had come to fish, that had been there to be witnessed to, came to the Lord a few years later. I don't know what happened with the rest of them. I only know that they cannot deny that a miracle happened that day.

Do you realize all that God went through for that young man to have a second chance to walk with Him? Do you realize that if I had not finally believed that it was the Lord asking me to go fishing that I would not have gone? Then, I had to get so sick that the boat came in hours early for this encounter to happen. The beginning of this encounter was in a prison in Idaho, and it was 12/13 years later on the Oregon coast that the story ends! When the Lord had convinced me to go with the pastor and "Mr. Faithful" to witness to this group of people, I had a totally different expectation. I was not expecting a divine encounter with an ex-inmate from Idaho I had not seen in years!

Many times our expectations can actually keep us from what God wants. Our expectations (those things we perceive will or will not happen as a result of spontaneous obedience) without a continued listening and surrender to the Lord can keep us from experiencing the intimate fellowship that God has for us. Our expectations after hearing from the Lord, are not correct or even close to what God has planned many times. We tend to listen to God and respond to His speaking filtered through our learned expectations, instead of through trust and anticipation. Maybe we should "anticipate God" instead of having "expectations of God."

I have learned many lessons from this experience and continue to use it to teach about God's grace, mercy, and love. It takes trust to see things like this happen. Walking and doing work with the Lord builds trust. What if I had been so centered on my expectations of how God was going to witness to the people on the boat that I became discouraged by being sick and had gone to the car and not been by that pole? What if I had doubted that Father had told me this young man was backslidden and had not spoken to him? So many times in my life, God's voice is just a thought or notion that comes to me. Through the years of walking with Jesus, and experiencing some truly outrageous incidents, I have started to learn to ask myself a different question when I get strange thought or pictures in my head. Instead of asking, "How could this be God?" I ask, "Why wouldn't this be God?"

That last encounter had covered about 12-13 years and a lot of living. Back in 1983, at the beginning of this encounter, I had already walked with the Lord many years even though I had been "in the church" only a couple of years. During that time, many of the experiences I encountered in my walk with the Lord, did not fit what formal traditional Christianity taught as the way God operated today. What knowledgeable believers and leaders told me didn't jibe with the scriptures I was reading, nor the experiences with God I have come to know. I have never been able to find the phrase "sit down" in the Word or the terms clergy/laity. I have never figured out how to live my Christianity one day a week or only in meetings sitting and listening to one man talk the whole time. We are supposed to go and do. I am as radical for the Lord as I had been in my life before He became my Lord. I have always been an adrenalin junkie, riding horses that were not always safe, riding motorcycles in the desert, working on jobs that were risky, and generally just being a rebel to what most people call normal life. A lot of my life has not been conformed to the "status-quo" of most of my friends. Sitting was not and is not really an option that appeals to me. I believe as I read the scriptures, you must live on the edge if you want to experience God to the fullest. All you have to do is simply read the epic journeys that most of these "God-men" lived and be hungry and passionate for what they had. You will have to trust, take risks and then- **GO**- to find the life of Christ we read about that He wants us to live!

What You Say is What You Get

> Listening should be the foundation of all our prayers. It is the language of caring and Love.

We were involved in a little charismatic church in Mountain Home, Idaho, for a few years in the early 1980's, and during this time we had some pretty radical meetings. One time, we were having a weekend of ministry at the church and several of us "wild bunch" type people were sharing testimonies. There were not appointed speakers, nor a time limit on the meetings. We just came and started to sing praises, and then follow whatever the Lord wanted to do. We were simply too "un-churched" to know that we had to have an "order of service" or agenda to follow, so we simply prayed and obeyed. We did not have any idea what we were doing.

During one of the worship times, a young lady stood up in the back to ask for prayer. Her husband had taken their four children and had gone back to Mexico with them. Since he was the father there was nothing the law could do. After he got to Mexico, he called his wife and told her she would not see her children ever again. She was broken. As the church prayed for her, I felt the Lord tell me to speak to her. As I faced her and finally got everyone to be quiet, I spoke, "Listen, the Lord told me that whatever you pray right now is exactly what will happen." Her reply was, "I simply want my kids back in the USA." I responded, "Listen, are you truly listening? Listen to exactly what the Lord is saying, because that is what will happen. He is saying that EXACTLY what you say in prayer is what will happen. So, do you want your husband saved and back with your kids in Mountain

Home, or what exactly do you want?" Again, she replied that she simply wanted her children back in the States. That day she received a call from the border patrol, and her husband had brought her children to the border and gave them her name and number and left them. This was EXACTLY what she prayed in response to the Lord's words to her. It cost the church a bit of money to go and get the children at the border and to bring all of them back home. I wonder what would have happened if she had asked for more? What if she had really heard what the Lord said? I found it amazing what happened and the church was thrilled. And yet, I was wondering why she asked for them to just be brought back to the US?

Where did that word come from, (I mean, how did I receive it) and what made it different than others I have spoken? How was it that I heard so clearly and exactly what I had spoken to her came to pass? I have found that the more I simply react to the Spirit of the Lord's impressions, the closer I am to hearing what the Lord is actually saying. I am not saying that everything I think is the Lord. I am saying that most of us operate in a place of insecurity that demands we have at least two or three confirmations before we will speak what we think the Lord is saying. The result is that the Word will be changed because of our reasoning and fretting about being accepted or rejected by those around us. I find that at times I still will compromise for the sake of what I think is keeping unity or being acceptable to everyone. The results are that what I speak and say differently than what is given to me, loses the anointing of Holy Spirit.

This time though, I had no fear or need to be accepted and simply spoke what was in my heart. This word that I gave actually changed me a lot. I realized that God could use me far more than I was willing to walk if I would stop rationalizing in my mind what I heard in my spirit. He also taught me something about trust; that our trust in Him is the most important aspect we have to show the reality of our relationship with the Father, and real heart trust changes what happens when God speaks. Here is another thought - God trusts us to listen. In growing into God's man or woman we must come to a greater place of communication skills and then trust. We must realize that to stay the same, year after year, is to be dead. A statue is steadfast, unchangeable, withstands all the elements, never strays, but has no life. Change is always a part of life, and listening is especially necessary in a relationship.

The Fear Factor

> The Gospel mandate is impossible without the Gospel power. Jesus needed the miracles to confirm the Gospel. Does He expect us to be convincing without them?

One time I was assembling a big irrigation machine in Idaho. At one point in the process of setting up this machine we had a crane holding up the center section with a chain while we attached various parts and pieces to it so it would stand by itself. The machine is 13 feet tall and I was up on it on one side fastening some parts to it. At the top of this machine is an 8 inch pipe about 14 feet long running parallel to the ground and supporting this pipe is a latticework frame. It is an upside down V- shaped network of angle iron connecting the pipe to machine framework. The whole machine weighs about 5 tons.

As I was working, my position was such that my stomach was centered on the end of this pipe and my upper torso was above it. As I watched, the chain holding this section of the machine came apart. (I need to insert here that I have no idea how this could happen since the chain was tight holding the machine in place for us to hook up all the attachments.) The chain came loose and I was staring at it in a flash of time, realizing that the machine was going to fall and I was on the wrong side in the wrong place. The man operating the crane remembers me saying **"Jesus"** rather loudly as the thing started to fall toward me. The pipe, where my stomach was positioned, sticks out about a foot further than the rest of the machine and when this thing came to rest, that pipe end would be buried one foot under the ground. The latticework below the pipe, that I was mentioning, has a hole in the end of it that at the wide part of the upside down V is about 36 inches, and it narrows to 8 inches at the top. I was standing with my feet on the bottom of the latticework and with my stomach at the pipe level when the machine started to go. When everything came to rest and the dust settled, I was standing up _under_ the 14 foot of pipe that is now pointing toward the sky inside the latticework frame. I had not a single bruise, no torn clothes, and no hole in my stomach. I was in a place impossible to get to. The 14-foot of pipe was now standing on end reaching toward the sky behind my back and I was standing under it inside the latticework wondering what had happened. I don't know how God got me there. I don't know how I was without a single scratch or torn clothing. I don't know why I was not totally shaken in fear, but I modestly crawled out of the network of bracings that surrounded me, walked out into the field a little ways, fell to my knees, and began to worship God for a little bit.

Those who witnessed this event were quite impressed with the fact that I was alive. One was the Mormon man studying to become a Bishop whom I mentioned in an earlier testimony. He came to me again and said, "I know that you should be dead, I know that what happened had to be God, but what I don't understand is why He continues to save you- because you go to the wrong church!" This man never did get what the Father was trying to show him; that he was the one going to the wrong church. I had no fear at the time, none! The whole incident still amazes me, and still this incident opens doors for me to witness to a whole lot of folks about the reality of God, and His miracles in the work place. Having God show up in your work place and doing things that astound those around you is a great way to change communities and what people feel about God. So many people are looking for God, but don't see reality in the visible Christian practices that are shown to the public. But when you live in the place of the miraculous at work and home you open the door for them to find what they are hungry for, and what you long to live—life in Christ.

Conclusion: If God is for us, who can be against us? What should we fear— only not knowing HIM! To be God's man, you must go through "stuff" that will either break you or deliver you from your fears and doubts.

By now you may realize that I tend to be a little unorthodox in my approach to Christianity and my walk may be a bit strange at times. Yet I think that many of us go through "stuff" and don't realize that it is Father's hand taking us to these tests and through them showing us our heart and helping us find freedom through the encounters.

Intimacy with the Lord is not something you can chant your way into, or pray enough to receive. This close relationship is not something that you can demand. It is a place filled with confidence as you live, that doesn't need to boast or flaunt itself. It is a place of knowing without thought for consequences. It is a place where your actions don't even have to be premeditated. Intimacy with Father is a place of position and power that breeds confidence and assurance in your actions and destroys fear. It is a place where risk is no longer risk because you know in whom you trust.

Fearlessness is a part of a close relationship with the Lord. It is acquired by going through places that require great trust. Fearlessness never walks alone; it is always in the company of love and faith. It allows the expression of love without the fear of rejection. God truly is fearless in His expression of love. He knows His love will not fail.

Fear cannot exist in the presence of assurance and confidence, but confidence does take time to cultivate. God knows that love will never fail because He is Love and He never quit being Himself. Fear does not exist in God, only in man. Intimate fellowship with Father destroys fear's right to exist. Taking risks and becoming close to Father will always cause us to have to deal with fears. To overcome fear, we must trust.

I have so many examples of fearless actions in my life, but none of them were planned. It was not that I did not have fear, I just reacted fearlessly. Situations happen, and I react or move in these times in ways that astound me and cause me to look back and marvel at the assurance in my actions. I think that fearlessness is a grace that stems from our position in Christ and His Kingdom. Satan knows when we know who we are. He also knows when we don't know who we are! Fear and deception are his greatest allies. Fear is what produces most of our yelling and extravagant gestures when we are confronted by evil. We think that if we are loud enough, we will scare the demons into obedience. We think our loudness is a sign of our power, but it generally is a sign of our fear of not being heard or obeyed. It shows our lack of authority, not our abundant authority. It shows our insecurities. It is not the loudness of our speech that changes things, but the boldness of our love.

One time, while up in the hills of Idaho praying and fasting for the bonds of wickedness in my life to be broken, I had an interesting encounter. It was cold up in those hills, and along the edge of the road was a couple of feet of snow. Around the cabin I was in, there were drifts about three to four feet high. I was alone in this place with no vehicle or phone for three days and nights. On the second day, in the afternoon, I was moved by the Lord to walk the road. God had me studying Isaiah, and I was finding some new thoughts as I read. So, while meditating on these scriptures, I set out for a walk.

Not far down the road, I came upon another cabin and there was a loose German Shepherd dog out front. As I walked by, this dog starts to run toward me barking and growling. I did not see him because he was just a little behind me when he began his attack. I am not sure what set him off. I am a little hard of hearing, have been my whole life, so I did not hear him coming until he was very close. As I turned, I saw him about 15 yards from me and he was coming at a run. In that instant of turning and seeing, I heard this word come out of my mouth with great strength, not yelling, but with a resonating assurance, "Sit, in Jesus Name!" I found I was also pointing at him with my finger. The dog slid to a stop about one foot from me and sat on his haunches, whining. I turned and walked off down the road. My adrenaline was not even pumping; I do not like big dogs that are angry and in most cases this would have brought me great panic. Amazingly, I was breathing normally and walked away continuing my conversation with God.

About a half mile down the road, I turned to come back, and as I turned and looked back up the road the way I had come, the dog was still sitting there. Getting closer again, I could see that he was still in the same spot. Then I saw the owner coming out and I heard him calling his dog, but the dog was just looking down the road at me, not paying any attention to his owner. The man came off his porch out toward the road, still hollering at his dog, who was not responding at all. It was still just staring at me. As I drew near, about a hundred yards from the dog, the owner of the dog reached the road and was actually trying to drag his dog back to the house. When he would let go of the dog's collar, it would run right back to the middle of the road and sit back down and stare down the road at me. He dragged his dog off the road several times with the same ending. By that time, he had seen me and was looking at his dog - then me - then back at the dog in wonder. I was closing the gap and speculating what would happen as this angry owner and I met, with his dog sitting and staring at me, still whining. The man stands up beside the dog, and as I passed they both were staring at me. When I got past them I felt that I needed to turn and release the dog. It was just a feeling, but I knew it was God. So I turned and quietly said, "Ok, you may go." That dog jumped up, still whining, and ran up the driveway to his home and rushed under the porch. The man was still standing there staring at his dog, and then me, alternately.

When I got to the cabin, I was filled with laughter at the experience. I know that dog was going to attack me. I also know that it was Holy Spirit that gave me the voice and control of that dog. That dog sat in that one spot for a good 25 minutes or so, never moving, as I walked down the road and back with Father. Even when dragged by his owner, he came back to the spot where I had told him to "sit." I have received a few revelations from this experience at various times as I shared it with others, but in reality, it was just a God-thing. I was with Him talking and walking and fear was not to be a part of my relationship with Him. I never even thought of being afraid. It just never occurred to me during the incident. Amazing! This was one more time when Father was increasing my ability to trust Him in the future. God is good, all the time! *The Bible tells us of Jesus' authority and the authority of the believer, but it is when the relationship and the scripture come in line, that we see the reality.*

Living While Waiting

> Practice makes permanent. You never outgrow your need for the basics. Just because you know the facts, doesn't mean you know the Truth.

Waiting on the Lord has more to do with serving than sitting, so for a period of time in my thirties, I would get up early, pray, and listen for Him to guide me to the place where someone would be willing to receive Jesus that day and then go wherever I felt led to through the pictures, thoughts, or addresses that came as I prayed. (I picked this up while reading about Smith Wigglesworth.) I always had this thought that whatever anyone else had done in Jesus, Jesus would do with me, if I was willing to pay the price they had. This praying for one soul a day had been going on for quite a few mornings, and I had seen someone saved nearly every day. (To have this happen, you must "hear" from the Lord and trust that what you hear is from the Lord, not just go about doing your own thing and asking the Lord to bless it.)

This particular morning I was lying on the floor praying and asking once more for a soul, "There must be someone who needs what I have to offer and who can receive the Gospel from me, Lord." Instead of giving me the name of a place in my mind or a picture like He had been doing, He *took me up above the earth,* [Now here is an expression that may be a bit confusing. How did He do that? Well, all I can say is that I left my body in some way and was in some kind of vision or realm where I was traveling with the Lord looking down on parts of the earth. I could not see the whole earth at once, but I could see the curvature and the land, like being in a glass bottom jetliner. The whole experience of traveling around the world took maybe ten minutes of actual time, though it seemed to last for hours].

In this spiritual journey, He started by showing me the northwest part of the USA. He asked me, "What do you see?" I replied, "Fires, little fires all over the area." He stated that I would start those fires. He said that I would kindle a flame, and that others would come and feed the fires that were started. Then He proceeded to take me on an around-the-world trip in the Spirit. In many countries that we passed over I would see little fires spring up. When I asked what they were, He told me that these were countries I would visit and start fires in. As we traveled over the globe, there were many countries He would point out with fires in them. He gave me a list of countries, as we went, that would be affected by what He had for me to do and share.

The Lord told me the vision I had seen would start with a phone call. As a result, I had a hard time from 1983 until 1999 being away from a phone. I was always afraid I would miss **the call**—kind of stupid. It was not like God didn't know where I was at any given time. I am sure He still knows my address!

Side bar---do not become consumed by a Word from the Lord. It is His Word. You cannot bring it to pass. You will only become frustrated if you attempt to fulfill something in the flesh that only the Spirit can complete. Your job, when given a Word, is to surrender, and like Mary, hide these sayings in your heart. Walk with God. Get to know Him and learn to trust Him. (I wish someone had told me this when I got the word I have just written down. That was information I could have used yesterday!)

When I told my friends about the vision, thinking they would be excited for me, I found most, if not all of them, laughed at me behind my back. I guess it did appear a little lofty to those who knew me, I suppose. After all, **they knew me**. As the years started going by and nothing happened, I grew disappointed, but I could not get away from the vision. I know that most of my friends were waiting for me to realize that I had been deceived, yet none of them actually condemned me for my dream. With so much prophecy being given in the Body of Christ at that time, and much of it never coming to pass, I can see why they did not believe what I had told them. Those first years of my total commitment to the Lord were filled with miracles and wonders, but I was not known by anyone and did not get invitations to do anything "big" that would get me started on the vision that Father had given me. It was a very frustrating period for me. I couldn't do anything to make it come to pass.

We moved several times, following the Lord, and having jobs doing electrical work that I did for provision. After a few moves, and much learning through the situations we encountered- (Sometimes I am sure that I was bonked on the head by a 2x4 and that the Lord's fingerprints were on it.)- the Lord spoke that He would have to rebuild my ship because the one I was in was running with the wind and would crash on the rocks. I did not recognize that He was actually talking about me continuing to look for men's approval to see the fulfillment of His vision. I thought it was about the church we were attending that was going the wrong direction, but that was not what the Lord was saying.

I was always waiting for the phone call or for someone important to recognize my "great" calling so I could begin to walk out the vision He had given me. I was trying to manipulate people into calling me.

What I got was people staying away from our meetings in parks, community halls and churches, by the thousands. It could have been my pride that kept them from coming; it could have been the Lord, or both. We had deliverances and healings regularly, but no one who was "someone or anyone" seemed to notice, except those whom Jesus touched. I did some pretty weird things to try to get people to notice that I existed. Once, I stood on a hill in a park in Pocatello, Idaho, and did a John the Baptist thing, "Repent you sinners...." That whole series of meetings did not go over well!

When the phone rang during those days, I might try to tear a door off the hinges to get to that phone if I was outside or not close to it. I was paranoid about phones and no matter what I was doing, if it rang, I would jump and run to get that thing answered. I was a real mystery to our neighbors in those days, as I would go out into the fields around our house and shout and rant at the Lord any hour of the day or night. I would scream prayers to the Lord and cry saying, "Send me, I will go, here am I!" I know that the Lord loved my heart, but I am sure that at times He had to chuckle at my ranting.

When a few years had gone by since I had been given the vision, I thought, "After three days Jesus was raised from the dead, so after three years we should have been noticed and the phone call should come any time now." When that did not happen, I had a yelling fit with Jesus. (Some might even call what I did throwing a tantrum). I _demanded_ that what He had shared with me come to pass. For some reason it seems that I lost that yelling match, and in the midst of His silence that followed I repented for my attitude. (I am not sure what I did could be called true repentance because this would turn out to be a repeated process through the years).

After seven years, I took my bibles and books and put them in a box and threw them in the garbage can. I figured that would make God sorry he had messed with me! I ranted and raved for a few hours and pouted for days. When I finally realized that my manipulation was not working (Father can speak so loudly in His silence), I went out, took my books out of the trash, and went back to praying and studying. Father would not be manipulated by my tantrums or my threat of quitting. He would not move like I wanted. Sometimes He just does not have a very good sense of humor about our selfishness, either! I continued doing a lot of loud praying at night in fields, in our home, yards, barns and at work. **Warning:** *This kind of prayer is not conducive to have others join you for conversation, or fellowship, after they have listened to you rant and rave with God for a period of time. It is just not very attractive.*

At times it seemed that my whole life was one big prayer, even though some of it could have been quieter. It all came from the hunger in my heart. I prayed that Father would send me to the lost, use me up doing your will, send me to places no one else would go, take my life and let others live. I prayed radical prayers like, "I want to know the fellowship of Jesus' suffering and the power of His resurrection." "I want to feel what your heart feels for the lost and the hurting." "Break me, mold me, use me, destroy me, I want to live hidden in Christ." "Destroy anything that stands between You and me. Whatever it takes or costs; I don't care, just do it!" <u>Unless you really want to know Jesus,</u> ***do not*** pray those kinds of prayers, because God will hear them!

During all these years, it wasn't like we were sitting around. We had Bible studies and groups meeting in our house and were doing youth groups and some ministry in churches. I was always discipling someone. We had a prison ministry and jail ministry going on in partnership with another ministry and also on our own. We were busy going and learning. Someone was always at our house being discipled or set free and prayer meetings were a common thing. In prisons we saw a man raised from the dead along with several other healings and deliverances (Maybe I will include an explanation of these in a future book). We were determined not to waste the trials that came our way, nor the time we had to live, so we were always set to learn more about Him and His desires through our life experiences, good or bad. We were constantly asking, "What should I be learning through this?" Dana has a saying, "Don't waste a good trial, you can learn something along the way." I hated the saying, but recognized that we needed to do just that; learn, grow and go. We had a few discussions with church leaders who thought I should sit down under them and learn more before we did what we were already doing. I would ask for scriptures that explained why I should sit and not "go make disciples", and preach the Word? Not a single one was able to bring scriptures that confirmed to me that waiting meant *doing nothing* or that I should *sit down*. Through this time, while I was "waiting on the Lord," I could not get away from the vision that was in me. I would try to be submissive to leaders, but when it came to disobeying scripture or putting down my vision, God's vision in me, I just could not do it. I spent an average of 2-5 hours a day in the Word or prayer and ministering to someone, besides working eight hours a day at my job. I was not a very good father to my sons, but it was not Jesus' fault, it was mine. My family suffered and experienced all that I did, and many times I did not even notice their pain.

It was a hard and wonderful time. At the end of ten years (since the vision had been given) I literally burned all the prophecies that

70

had come. (Wherever I went, strangers and Christians continued to prophesy over me great words and anointing, the double portion of Elisha, and that I would minister to multitudes, etc., etc., blah, blah, blah). I put all those words I had written down in a can and set fire to them. It was done, finished. I knew I had been deceived, but now I could go on with living, free at last! My friends had been right. Nothing I tried seemed to be able to bring the vision in my heart and head to reality! How was I ever going to get overseas if no one noticed me? I completely gave up on it all; put my books up, and sat down. That lasted about 12 hours until I received the mail. A lady we had not seen for 5-6 years wrote me a letter. (In the midst of my tantrums God did have a sense of humor!!) What timing! She was an intercessor, sold out to the Lord, and had been praying when the Lord put it on her heart to pray for us. She was told to write down what she saw and send it to me.

Everything I had thrown away was in that letter, the whole vision and all the prophecies. (It came just twelve hours after I had burned all the evidence of the vision and all the prophecies given me over the years.) Even some of the same scriptures that I had been given by the Lord were in her letter. That is just not right! God resourcefully resurrected what I had emphatically thrown away. The Father just does not play fair! It made me so mad, but it also made me laugh. Here I was trying to manipulate the Father and what does He do, but have someone send me a letter that is impossible for a person to write. What an amazing God! He did not forsake me, but instead sent me a letter and encouraged me to get up and go on. So life went on, and I surrendered to never getting away from "the vision." It was a part of me. It always has been. It just got frustrating at times feeling that nothing was happening to move me toward the fulfillment of it.

I know this is not true, things were happening. The problem was that I did not want to be surrendered, nor see what He was saying. We people are big on keeping some control of our lives. Everything that happens in our lives can shape us for His vision of our lives if we will allow Him to use all things. We need to value all of life, not just the good times, because there are lessons to learn from all we go through. Before we left Moses Lake, WA, we had seen so many wonderful things in the prison/jail ministries we were involved in and with the youth at the Job Corps where we worked. Our home had been a revolving door. We had some struggles at a couple of churches. I had close ties with several pastors in the area that I met with for accountability and those relationships continued, in spite of the attacks of some of the more religious leaders in the area. It was a time of testing and wonderful grace and a time that caused us to dig into the Word and check ourselves out to make sure we were not being deceived or divisive, unintentionally.

This period was a time of humbling, also, as God had told us not to defend ourselves during all that went on. He told us that if we had to put others down to clear our name, we would lose His presence and favor. In other words, if we defended ourselves, we would be out of His will and place ourselves in a place that He would not be able to deal with others, but would have to deal with us in some way that might not be fun to live through.

It was always interesting to us that those who came against us, reaching out in prisons and on the streets or with various youth groups, never brought any biblical reasons to show us that we should quit what we were doing. They would just be upset at us and want us to sit down! <u>Disapproval by other leaders does not prove you are walking close to Jesus.</u> Never let rejection be the sole evidence or

72

sign of your closeness to Father. We all can mis-hear and miss the mark. We have need of judging ourselves rightly and to be willing to see what the Word actually says and hear what you are actually do- ing. Deception works well with arrogance and pride.

I like to live in intimate fellowship with the Lord and live out His presence in me everywhere I can. When you spend time with the Lord, not to get something from Him but just to be with Him, you cannot help but know things about some people's lives and needs without being told these things by them because that is what Jesus is about. He knows the heart of all people and at times will reveal some peoples' heart to you as you walk through life. He wants you to pray for them or reach out and touch them. Many times I have had inci- dents at work or in restaurants where the Holy Spirit will tell me something or show me something about someone. I will go up to them and ask them a question, ask to pray for them or speak some- thing into their lives from the Lord. In all the situations we have gone through with church groups and others, God was there giving me words, encouragement, and showing me things to come in our lives. In some cases, I would know exactly what was going to happen at some meeting or at work before I left the house. I made myself vulnerable to listen and I expected when I asked Jesus a question that I would receive an answer. I don't look for a specific answer, just an answer.

In most incidents, when we Christians have asked our Father or Jesus a question, the problem with our receiving an answer is that we are not willing to hear or don't know how Jesus speaks. So we don't know where to look for His answer. I will give you an example.

During our time in Moses Lake, Washington, the Lord had laid it on my heart to start a youth group on the Job Corp site where I worked.

I put out flyers and had gotten cookies, snacks and games for the youth to play. I was set. The first night, the kids came and ate the goodies and then left. They did not stay for me to speak or to pray. They came to eat and play, but they were not interested in anything to do with God. This went on for some time, and I was pretty discouraged. I knew God had said to start a group, but no one was coming after the initial couple of meetings. After a bit, I quit going. I told the Lord it was not working and that I was through. But, I could not get away from God speaking to me, through my feelings for these kids, that I needed to start a youth group on the center. I could not get the thought out of my mind. It kept me in unrest for weeks after I quit trying to have meetings. Dana finally spoke to me one night, "God told you to go and you are making us all miserable. You know you are in sin by not going, so please go..." (Sometimes I think it would be nice if she were wrong just once!)

I put out some more flyers and started the meetings again. No one showed up for two weeks, so it was just God and me for an hour, praying and talking together. Actually, I was complaining more than praying, because no one was coming. I kept asking Him, "What do You want from me?" I had snacks, games, goodies, and door prizes, and yet no one came.

After a couple of weeks of absolutely no one showing up I cried out, "I have done all I know how to do!" At this point, Father broke in, "That is right, YOU have done all YOU know!" I got the point, I had not really asked Him what to do, and I had not taken the time to listen after asking. I had just assumed that I should do what others had taught me about how to do youth groups. Many times we hear God tell us to do something, but we don't stay with Him long enough to see _how_ to do what He tells us to do. In the silence I waited, but

74

nothing more came, and I asked forgiveness for not asking or listening more, and then left. As I was on my way back to my car, a young man that was a student in the trade that I taught, walked up asking why I was there at night. I was an instructor during the daytime hours, so for me to be on the campus during the evening hours seemed strange to this young man. I responded that I was there to do some youth meetings, and then out of my mouth came, "The next one is just for you." I had no pre-thought to that, it just came out. God gave me the words as I opened my mouth. "Really," he replied. "Yes, it is just for you, and it starts at 7 pm Thursday night." I got there early, and was praying, when finally about 7:15 or so this young man comes in, looks around and makes the comment, "I thought you said you were holding youth meetings." My reply was, "Yes, and I said that the next one was just for you." He looked around at the empty room again and turned to go. I watched as he held the door open, and then as he slowly turned asking, "What would we do?" "You pray, and I will agree," was my reply. He closed the door and came toward me saying he didn't know how to pray. My reply was, "Yes, you do. Everyone knows the Lord's Prayer, start with that." He looked around, sat down and folding his hands recited the Lord's Prayer. I said, "I agree". He started again, but as he spoke, I noted a change in the tone of his voice. Soon he was saying it again and had knelt down on the floor. Then he was confessing his sins to Jesus and crying. Next he was lying on the floor in tears as he renounced all his past, all the evil he had done, and not only did he surrender to Jesus, but he got filled with the Spirit of God! This went on for an hour or more. He prayed and I would say, "I agree."

Finally, it was over and he was getting ready to leave. I told him that the first person he touched would get knocked down, and he was to tell them, "It is just Jesus; I have been in His presence." I told him not to be afraid because it would be a sign to him to confirm what had happened to him. As I headed for the car, I was thinking about what had happened and that what I had told him was crazy. I was smiling to myself at what had taken place and wondered what would happen next. As I arrived at my car and was getting ready to leave, I heard this young man yelling for me to wait. He came running up to me with another young man who wanted to receive Jesus. As I recall, the young man I had been praying with was walking up the stairs to his dorm room and touched the other one and he was knocked down. The youth that had been doing the prayer time with me told the guy who was knocked down, "It is just Jesus." The fallen kid responded, "I want what you got," so the young man brought him to my car before I could even leave for home. I refused to bring this kid to the Lord, and told the young man who had prayed for so long, and had encountered Jesus, to do it. I left them there on the sidewalk on their knees, one leading the other to the Lord. In six months, we saw approximately fifty or more young adults receive Jesus through His power and presence, and a multitude more were witnessed to through His miraculous presence in those young people. It was a grand time and signs and wonders were common.

My intimacy with the Lord is neither a "practice" nor a "program." I don't turn it on for "Christian activities" and then off at work or play. It is real life, lived with the Master. If we will listen, HE will tell us how to reach the lost and show us His plan as we daily walk with Him. Listen and then obey... I taught all those young people they could hear the voice of God and that Christianity was a real relationship, not a religious rite from the beginning. They took the scriptures I used in teaching them, and went out and did it. They simply started to live in relationship with Jesus, and they saw so many miracles, and had so many divine words for other kids, it was amazing to watch. I did not preach at them, instead I would question them and bring up a scripture and let them tell me what it meant. They would read the scripture, pray over it, and ask the Holy Spirit to show them what it meant, then they would write down what they got and come share it with the group. They began to live what they found. What a time we had! I am still in contact with several of those young people, and they still hear God's voice... they are making a difference in their world because Jesus made a difference in them.

We were also ministering in a maximum-security prison at the time. While doing a meeting with about 40 inmates, an old man fell over dead while I was teaching. (I have often wondered if I simply bored him to death). The younger Christians in the place were praying for him to receive Jesus. (He never missed a meeting but did not know Jesus.) I had taught them to live radically for the Lord, and we had seen some miracles in the prison before. This was a different story, I didn't know what to do with a dead man. When we checked him out and found no pulse, the guys gathered around him saying, "This is not right! We have been praying for him to become a believer and now he dies without Jesus? No way!" I was at the door trying to get a guard's attention so they could come remove the dead guy, and these brothers were praying for him to come back to life so he could receive Jesus. I had never raised anyone from the dead, nor had I seen it at that stage in my life. Once I got a guard's attention, I came back over and joined them. The guard brought a medical team about 15 minutes later, they checked his heart and pulse, then lifted him onto a gurney and put a sheet over him. They took 10 minutes in just getting out of the room, and no one was working on him or excited in any way.

About 20 minutes later the door opens again, and in walks this old man, with a big smile on his face, and all the medical staff and guards entered with him. They stayed until the meeting ended, and the old man just sat and smiled the whole time. There were some excited brothers in that room, but with the guards presence, it was pretty subdued excitement. Two weeks later this old gentleman received Jesus, and a few weeks after that he passed on to heaven... Awesome!

I had so many experiences through the years that were all founded on my intimate communion with the Lord- hearing His voice and simply obeying. I don't know how I know it is God at times, but then if I am praying and asking Him something, why would it be anyone else that answers? If I am ministering and sharing about Him, why wouldn't it be Him who puts thoughts and words for others and actions to take in my head? If your heart is to know Him, why would He not make Himself known? The more you walk with Jesus as a friend and desire to know Him, the easier it gets to recognize who is talking, just like in any other relationship you pursue.

In around 1985, I was in a county jail doing a weekly service. In this jail, we had both men and women from different pods or multi-cell units together in the service. The only time that all these people in different pods or units could get together to talk was in chapel. I was alone this day doing the service and there were about fifty inmates in the room with me. As is normal, no guard was in the room with me and it was just the inmates and me in a locked room together. Everyone was a little rowdy, and I had one man who was always a troublemaker in the meeting. He did not like me, as I had confronted him a time or two in the past, and he had been put back in his cell as punishment for stirring up trouble in the meetings. I always allowed him to come back to chapel services after a period of time of being out of our meetings, thinking that sooner or later he would receive the truth. This day he was causing a lot of contention, and there were many with him who decided that I was not going to be preaching. They were going to visit, play games, and simply ignore me. When I started to speak, they would howl or do all sort of things to disrupt me, including telling me to shut up. I finally gave up and sat down on a stool that I had in front and waited for the Lord to show me what to do. After a moment, I got up, took my Thompson Chain Reference Bible and threw it against a wall forcefully. The papers in it went flying everywhere, and the Bible slid down the wall to the floor. I turned and quietly said, "Let's not use that today." You could have heard a pin drop as I sat on the stool and looked around. Every eye was on me, and there was still not a sound. Softly I said, "Let's talk about my Jesus today," and I did. I just talked to them and let them ask me questions as I simply enjoyed sharing about my love for Jesus. As I was sharing, the man who always caused trouble started to cry, went over to the wall where I had thrown my Bible, picked it and the papers scattered everywhere up, and put it all back together. He even straightened the pages. At the end of the meeting, a young man came up and told me that he was being extradited to Washington D.C. the next day for a trial and wanted to receive Jesus right then. He said that he had never heard about Jesus the way I shared that day. He was convicted that Jesus was his only hope. I prayed with him and then the meeting was over. A week or so later, when I was visiting some of the brothers in their cells, the troublemaker from the meeting came to me, and after talking a bit, had me pray for him to received Jesus. He was changed. The two of us had some good Jesus times in the jail meetings after that, and he would always make sure that everyone was quiet and respectful. It was an awesome transformation to watch.

Intimate fellowship with the Lord is exciting and so easy if you trust the One you are praying to. Sometimes it does not seem wise to do the things He says to do, but the proof is in the fruit. I have made many mistakes and missed it entirely, yet I have also been thrilled, amazed, and encouraged as I continue to learn how to hear and be selflessly obedient. Father does show me where I am and continuously makes sure I recognize He is God and I am not.

Which child do you talk the most to, the one who is being obedient or the one you feel is in trouble or has missed something? Why do we think that when we miss it God stops talking or when we are in sin we cannot hear God?

Discipling: Living in Intimacy

If we ask Jesus, "What do you want us to do?" shouldn't we also ask how, when, and where?

We should teach who God is, who we are, what we must do, what He has done, and then what He promises.

I am always looking to make disciples and I am always looking for someone who is hungry to go do something rather than someone waiting for something to do. I take them with me and get them doing things they would not think they could do. I feed their desire to see Jesus move in their lives and find a way to empower them to see their dreams begin to take on real life. If we are about Jesus' desires, we will find Him. As we lose our lives for others we find our life in Him. We are to "Go" make disciples according to Mt. 28:18-20. That is one of the main functions of our lives.

Each day I look for ways to feed some Christian's desire to know Jesus better. Discipleship is imperative, and it is a command. It is simple to accomplish, and wonderful to watch the results of it in people's lives. True discipleship brings people to a place of freedom and fruitfulness in Christ. We call Mt. 28:18-20 the "Great Commission," but few do it with the goal of loosing someone else to walk "just like Jesus." Some do it to keep control "over someone," but few do it to release and free someone into an intimate close fellowship with Father. Most of our discipleship is to get someone to conform to our walk or doctrines. Jesus has only one goal, and that is to get people into a place where they hear the voice of their Father and walk in the position of being one with God (Jn. 17:17-23.).

81

In the midst of this time of great miracles, awesome ministry, adversity and turmoil that were going by so fast, God told us that we were to move to the mountains. We were ministering in prison, county jails, the Job Corps, and in parks and any place else we found ourselves. We had two families living with us in a three bedroom duplex. Our son, Phillip, had a junior-high group meeting in our home, and Bible studies and prayer meetings were going on constantly. It seemed crazy for the Lord to say "move" while we were seeing such fruit being produced for His kingdom, so we had a hard time leaving it behind and obeying His call.

The Lord showed us that if we stayed, the people we had trained would not step up and become who they were called to be. So we surrendered, moved, and left the work we were doing in other's hands. Many of our friends disagreed with what we did. They could not see the Lord stopping what we were doing to move into obscurity when so many miracles were taking place. It was a hard thing to know what the Lord was saying and going against all the counsel we were receiving. Most felt that by leaving, we would be walking away from His presence into a place of death.

In Roseburg, Oregon, we found ourselves doing nothing! All the time the phone was right there, but it was not ringing. People were still staying away from meetings I spoke at or put on by the thousands. I knew we had not missed it, but it sure was different than the last 6-7 years had been. We moved into nothingness, and I was not a happy camper! How could we fulfill God's desire for us while we did nothing nor met anyone of significance to see we were an asset to Christianity not a curse? I could not imagine how I could start fires all over the world and the northwest when no one knew my address or phone number? (We are so funny sometimes when we think that God does not know our address or we feel that we are left out and God is ignoring us).

In Roseburg, we attended several churches over a period of time and had some good experiences, but there was not a lot going on with us. During the time I worked for the government as a trade instructor and electrician at two different Job Corp sites, my superiors sent me to several trainings on leadership and counseling. While I was attending their trainings on supervision, I was being trained for service with the Lord. God used those secular trainings to teach me more about servant leadership and unity. Most of my peers would get one training every two years. I would get three or four every year, and would not request any. I am sure that it was a God thing. As time went on, we did see some miracles happen in our new home, and we continually saw God's hand training us and leading us forward. During this time, one of the men I worked with came into my office one morning, and as he entered I had a thought go through my mind. Sometimes when God speaks it is just a strange thought appearing in my mind. I told this man, "You had a nightmare last night; do you want to tell me about it"? (That may not be the direct quote, but close.) He looked at me, and you could see he was stunned. He proceeds to tell me about this reoccurring nightmare he has had. I interpreted it for him after he finished and explained to him that God was talking to him and trying to save him. Through this and several other times that God would show me something about his life that I could not know, he gave his heart to the Jesus. It was always fun to watch the expression on his face when I would speak something I should not know.

On one occasion we went to visit some friends of ours who lived in the state of Washington. We were going somewhere to do some ministry, and since we were passing through the area they lived, we had set up an appointment to meet them at a restaurant. When we got there and entered the restaurant with them, I noticed a young couple sitting beside each other at a booth near the entrance. Before we got to our table I knew that I had to go speak to them. (At times I see someone and I get this strange feeling that I am to say something to them. The problem is that I don't know what I am to say or do.) I left my wife and friends and went to this young couple's table with a sense of anticipation and dread. As I sat down I started to speak, "You do not know me and my name is not important, the Father sent me over here to talk to you." Just imagine someone doing that to you and you will probably know the reaction I got from them. I know they thought I was "one fry short of a happy meal." Their silence said it all. I started, "You are both Christians and you attended different denominations before you were married. Since you got married you have not gone to church because you don't know which one to go to." The lady's eyes are starting to get big and the young man's mouth is beginning to drop open. "God has a plan for your lives, and He wants you back in fellowship! There is a church just around the corner from where you are living. Go there. It is not from either of your denominations." By this time, both of them were in tears. Several times during my speaking the young lady would ask, "How do you know this?" It was interesting; because I even told them which denominations they had been a part of before getting married. It was so amazing! Words were coming to my mind, and I was simply speaking them, and this couple was telling me that my words were true! I said some more to them about God's call on them, prayed over them and left them crying. When we left the restaurant thirty minutes or so later they were still crying and talking together. Part of being God's man is being willing to do a few crazy things. NOTE-- Not all crazy things are from the Lord. Many times we want to look good before others or show that we are "out of the box", so we will do "exhibitions of faith." Unfortunately, I have done a few of those, also. We do not need to do exhibitions to show faith; we need to be after His heart and have a willingness to trust and obey without a lot of fanfare or doubt. The truth of whether you are following God or self becomes apparent in the results -- which we cannot see, but will know one day.

Holy Spirit Speaking and the Resurrection Commands

> The difference between Biblical Christianity and religion is that Biblical Christianity possesses in substance what religion only has in words. The commands of Christ are not to be discussed, but obeyed.

There are so many scriptures in the Word about God speaking to men. Several times in the book of John, the Word shows us that the Holy Spirit will teach us or guide us into all truth, show us things to come and bring to our remembrance all things that Jesus has said. (Jn. 14:26, 15:26, 16:13) Why don't we see that happening in more Christian's lives? I think that one of the keys is that we do not teach as a foundation that an intimate fellowship with God and hearing the voice of God is normal Christianity.

We start in the wrong place as we place an emphasis on knowledge of the Bible and memorization of scripture. These are good things, but when they are the emphasis, and not the result of our time with Him, we are headed in the wrong direction. We major on minors and do not teach a foundation based on the things that Jesus thought were important when He left the yet-to-be-born church in the hands of the disciples. Instead of us edifying and equipping new believers to begin experiencing intimacy with Father the way Jesus modeled, we tend to teach knowledge as the foundation of our Christianity. In the Western mindset, for someone to be classified as mature, they must have lots of knowledge and a little experience. Jesus' disciples had lots of experience and a little knowledge. He left some basic commands at the end of each Gospel that should be our beginning point. Obedience to them should be the foundation that shows us how to fulfill the great commandments of love and the great commission to go. I believe that when we teach new disciples how to obey Jesus' resurrection commands, based on a familiarity and closeness to the Lord, and we then show them that they can hear God's voice, many more people will experience incidents similar to the one I have just finished describing that took place in the restaurant with the young couple in their everyday living.

In our children's education, we all have some basic commands that we reiterate through the years that we feel are very important for them to remember. When we come to the time that we are going to go away and leave them for the first time without any other supervision, even if it is for only an hour, before we leave, we will reiterate the most important commands for them to remember and practice while we are absent. One command that was a part of my life and our sons, was, "don't play with matches." We had wood stoves and matches were always around, so teaching the kids not to play with them and training them in the use of matches was very important. There were a lot of other things our sons learned in the 10-12 years before the moment of leaving them for a while alone, but to us, this was an important thing to remember. So when we were to leave them for a few moments I would reiterate what was important for them to remember, "Don't play with matches." I believe that Jesus' statements after He was resurrected are similar. Of all the things that He taught the disciples, these resurrection commands are the important ones to remember and practice first. He is reiterating His priorities for them to do in these commands before He leaves them. He is not telling them to forget the other things they know, but simply that these commands need to have pre-eminence.

The reason Jesus was sent to us was to be the example for us to follow and show us what it means to: preach the gospel (Jesus saves), heal the brokenhearted, proclaim liberty of the captives (to free from demonic activity), recovery of sight (to heal), to proclaim that now is the time, "the acceptable year of the Lord"(preach salvation). (Lu. 4:18). Jesus is sent to do exactly what He then sends his twelve disciples to do. Then, in the resurrection commands, He dictates to all His disciples (that includes us, Jn. 17:20) that we are to teach those that follow to do the same. Paul reiterates the same foundational priorities for all of us years later in Heb. 6:1-2. Somehow we should get the idea! Heart motivated obedience is the only sign we can give to Jesus and the world that we truly believe and love Him.

What would happen if we focused a new believer on doing Jesus' resurrection commands to show that He loves Jesus? (Jn. 14:15,21 and 15:14). The Kingdom of God would happen, that is what! These are the things that need to be the foundation of Christianity. All of them have to do with walking with Jesus, intimate fellowship, going and doing things together with Him. His resurrection commands are pretty simple and don't take a lot of knowledge, just faith, hope and love. These foundations and last commands should be the first principles taught and focused on. We think they are for the mature, but Paul says they are the foundation, and you can't go on to maturity without ("by reason of use") doing them (Heb. 5:11-14).

To conclude the story about talking into a couple's life (that I did not know), I really believe if we were to get the correct foundation into those we are around and have influence on, we would see what I did to the young couple in the restaurant repeatedly acted out in many believers' lives. We would change the world around us because we would be keeping the basic principles of Christ, which requires that we hear Him and live in Him, so we can obey in this age. God's people will be about great exploits which is the Gospel and which cannot be done without His guidance and presence every day. Guidance comes through an intimate relationship, not religious practices.

A few years back, I was with a friend of mine who wanted to learn more about hearing the voice of God. He was hungry to be used by the Lord. We met for a breakfast before his workday began. We had a few laughs together and encouraged each other in the Lord and I tried to get him to see that God was speaking to him. As we got up and started for the door, I noticed a lady and her daughter eating at a booth, and as we walked by, I heard the Lord say, "She needs prayer." As we continued to walk, I acknowledged His word to me with a "yes" in my spirit as I continued to talk with my friend. Again I heard, "She needs prayer." Ah, I was getting it. Here was an example for me to share with my friend who wanted to be used by the Lord. I stopped our conversation and returned to their booth. "As I walked by, the Holy Spirit nudged me and told me you could use some prayer. Can we pray for you?" The response was tears and a nod, because she lacked the ability to speak right then. After we prayed and she got control of herself, she told us this story. Her mother had retired and decided to move to the town we lived in. After selling her house and getting everything arranged, she moved into a retirement village in our small community. Everything was good until about four months later when she had a severe stroke. Her daughter lived in California and did not have the money or the way to come and stay with her often. Her family situation did not lend itself to bringing her mother back from Oregon to California. She would come up once or twice a week to see her mom, but to do so she had to take her own daughter out of school or find somewhere to have her go when not in school, as her husband's job was time-intensive. She was a Christian and had prayed over this situation, yet she was in despair, as she could not keep coming up, and there was no way to get her mom home. The night before, she had cried herself to sleep with this thought, "God, do you even care? Are you listening to me at all? I need to know you care and will work this out for me. I have done all I can do and there seems no way for me to be able to care for my mom and my family. Please show me you care and send someone to pray for me tomorrow." I received the spiritual nudge to pray for her as she was eating breakfast the next day! What if I had been too embarrassed to pray in public? And what about my friend who wanted to know about hearing God's voice and obeying? I got to share with him on the way to our cars about what happened and how he could do that also, if he would simply listen. What a great God and Father!

Continued Living While Waiting

> Faith is to be experienced, not memorized.
> If the life of faith is easy, then you aren't living the life of faith. Faith is the recognition of who Jesus is, and begins with a call to abandon oneself to the will and leading of the Lord.

Around the end of the '90's the Lord started to deal with me more radically, showing me how I had lived trying to please people whom I thought could help me unfold God's vision for my life. In several visions, He showed me all the past and the struggles we had gone through. He showed me His faithfulness and help in all the situations we had encountered over the years. He showed me my pride and arrogance, and then He showed me His love and humility.

One day while I was driving home, He told me that He was going to show me what **my** disobediences and attitudes had cost Him and His kingdom, and then what they had cost me and my family. In a moment of time I was so emotional that I could not drive, and desperately pulled onto the shoulder of the road and stopped. He showered me with remembrances and pictures that crushed me. Then He took me through them and showed me what I had done, what He had done, and the costs to both of us. To say the least, it shook me to the bone to see what I had destroyed or messed up. I appreciated the fact that in the midst of His sharing the truth with me He showed me how He had turned many of my disobediences to good, even though destruction happened in some instances. What He had wanted to happen did not take place. It took Him less than five minutes to cause me to cry like a baby and to see how stupid I had been, trying to live to please men and win their approval to carry out His vision. I broke and surrendered my future and my past to Him. I am not sure how long I sat there and cried and listened, but I know that He unfolded a lot to me, and it was a life-changing moment. It was instantly, emotionally too much, and it was also very personal. At the end of this time He showed me we were not through, and that He was for me and not against me by asking me a simple question, "Do you think that others have anything to do with the vision that I have shown you? Your fellowship and obedience to Me; your relationship with Me is what will fulfill My vision because it is mine, not man's!" At that moment, I completely lost my need of men's approval, (we are to be submitted to one another in the Lord and live in a place of humility and community) and gained a strength in my spirit that gave me instant peace. Gal. 1:10 took root in me and I was free. All the years that had gone by now made sense, and His education was starting to mold me in a new way, instantly. I found freedom in Christ and began to really **LIVE** for the audience of One, not just **SAY** I was. I gave up trying to be good enough for God to fulfill His desire in me, because I realized that this vision I was living for was His, and it was His desire for me. My part in this vision was to be concerned and focused on my intimate fellowship with the Lord. I needed to get to know Him more, up close and personally, and let the Father take care of the rest of it. Even though I had always been concerned with intimacy and discipleship, I was in a place of freedom that I had never experienced. I did not have to make God's vision come to pass any more, and I did not need the affirmation of men for it to come to pass or even if it came to pass! This thing was between God and me!

For the first time in my walk with Jesus I was excited about how the vision had brought me to this place of intimacy with the Lord and was thrilled with the daily working out of our relationship. I needed nothing more.

I turned fifty in the year of 2000. Seventeen years had gone by, and no phone call had come since I had had the vision of starting fires around the world. I was still waiting, and could not give up the vision any more than I could stop myself from breathing. My wife and I had come into agreement on the things we believed the Lord was saying to us for the coming year. Dana and I had sat down separately and made a list of what we felt God was saying, and then we took a trip away from home to have a quiet time to talk about these things and see where we were in agreement. We agreed we should sell the house, pay off all our bills and get ready to travel, though we had no idea why. We were to move to a small place and spend more time dwelling on His purposes for our future. It took us several months to get to this place of freedom we felt the Lord wanted us in, and when we had accomplished what He had put on our hearts to do, we went away together and prayed again. During that time of prayer, I told Dana that if God's vision didn't come to pass this year, while I was 50, that I was going to give up my vision. I would not live for it anymore, in any way. Even though I was truly grateful for the vision that had brought me to such a place of intimacy that I was walking in with the Lord, I would live for it no more. We were busy doing the Gospel, seeing the Lord move, and I no longer had the need for ministry to prove myself to God or others. We were praying, learning and ministering still, but I was not driven anymore by the vision God had given me, nor the need for approval of men. Praise God!

A few months later we had moved into a smaller home and decided we needed to once again take a time out and travel to the Oregon coast for a time of prayer. It was affirming, and we once again knew that we were right where we were supposed to be and drove home content with whatever the Lord had in store for us. When we arrived home, the phone was ringing as we exited the car. I did not rush to the house and tear the door down to get to the phone to answer it. Dana was impressed with the change and we actually were talking about it as we got into the house. I was not living for a phone call any longer. We put things up from our trip and finally I went to the answering machine to see who it was that had called. One of our friends, who was a board member in an international ministry, had called. He called again, and when I answered the phone, his first question was, "Neil, would you like to go to India with me?" He had no idea what my vision was nor did he know that India was the first country on the list God had given me 17.5 years before. I had not shared my vision for several years because most people just thought I was nuts and I had quit living for it.

In November of my 50th year, I went to India, the beginning place of God's vision for me! I landed in Kolkata on my first trip out of the USA, and I was so broken after the first 2 days there by what I saw, smelled and experienced, that I could not deal with what was happening. The beginning of the fulfillment of God's vision was not playing out as I had anticipated, thus I struggled to comprehend what I was experiencing. The first morning I saw a truck come down the street picking up those who had died on the street during the night. I saw despair and hopelessness everywhere I turned. The odors were overwhelming, and I had never seen poverty or despair like what was in front of me. During those first few days, I spent a lot of time broken, and when I thought of the vision God had given me I wondered how this could be the start of it? I feared that I would be let down again and life would continue to go on with nothing more happening. I had lived in the place of nothing happening in regards to my vision for so long, that I had lost faith, and held onto only a small hope for the future of the vision I could not get away from. Being in Kolkata the first few days did not help, as I had never seen helplessness and hunger like what I saw there. The Lord spoke to me and said this was the seat of Satan, not the city, but the place the people were in, with only hopelessness and the people living a meaningless existence. It was hard to accept that what I had dreamed was actually happening or that this could possibly be the beginning of me fulfilling the vision.

While in India, I was in the company of many national Christian leaders and ministries, and by the end of the trip, many of these leaders were asking me my opinion and what I thought on several fronts! This was so ridiculous and unreal for me at times that I would just laugh. One night, at one of these meetings, a Prophetess (Indian) and I were put together to talk for awhile. She had just gotten out of the hospital after being beaten up for sharing the gospel in a Muslim area. She and I were discussing why she was going back after they had abused her and had put her in the hospital. As we finished sharing, I had a word for her, gave it to her, and then prayed for her. We cried together a bit and then went to our cars to leave. We said good-bye, and as we were getting in the car she said, "Now it is my turn!" Here I was in India, almost 17.5 years after the initial vision that the Lord had given. I have had many people in the USA confirm and prophesy over me about this vision for years. Now in the year 2000, this Indian lady spoke the same words and scriptures over me that I had heard from the Lord all those years before in 1983. It was so amazing; I just stood there with everyone else and spoke nothing. Inside, I was speaking though, because I had developed this word through the years that I would think as people would begin to prophesy over me. "We will see!" I had stopped believing and all the "words" spoken over me were like hot air and I had gotten to the point that I would just say inside, "we'll see" as people would speak. I was tired of hearing about what I was to do when nothing was happening that I could see. Now, here I am in the midst of the first trip overseas and these words are being spoken that I had heard for so many years, with no action taking place, by an Indian lady who met me that night. As the thought started to go through my mind, she stopped speaking and stuck her finger in my face, "Don't ever say that again!" "Don't say 'we will see' ever again, for the time is now and you will see the vision start now!" I had said nothing, just thought it. Wow, was I undone! I had told her nothing about what she was saying even though all of it was true. The Lord had spoken profoundly once again!

After that first trip, I was back working and struggling with the reality of what had happened. Dana knew from looking at me and hearing the stories about India that we would move there. As an interesting change had happened in my heart, the fulfillment of the vision was something that, now, I didn't feel ready for. I was trying to avoid walking in what had ruled my life for so long. Many times in our walk with the Lord we pray for things or see things about our future and say, "Yes" to Jesus even though we don't have a clue what that something will be like. We preconceive the outcome of saying "Yes" and go on our way. Then out of "nowhere" God brings an opportunity to walk out our prayer or the thing we said "Yes" to. There is something wrong though; this thing or answer to our prayer does not look like what we thought we were praying for. The glory we thought would be in it for us is not there. We are disillusioned because our prayer or vision does not come to pass like we expected. Many times we miss God "Bringing to pass our vision or the desire of our heart" because we have pre-conceived how it should look. _It is the difference between expectation- which limits the alternative methods and endings- and anticipation- (which lives in a place of no boundaries as to what and how,) open and simply knowing that God is going to show up and do something to bring His Word to pass._

I was coming to grips with the fact that I had been hearing from the Lord all these years, and even though I knew it was the voice of the Lord: sharing, preparing, moving, strengthening, and breaking me, I now knew I was not ready because I had seen the vision coming to pass much differently than the Lord was now showing me. Knowing God and walking in intimate close fellowship with Him had been the goal of my life. To know His love and to have His heart was what I lived for. The vision He gave me in 1983 had been the cornerstone of strength I had needed to make it through so many trials, tribulations, good times and bad. Much of the intimate fellowship I experienced with the Lord had come from the preparation for this journey. Now as I was propelled into the vision of all these years, I felt totally inadequate to the task and that I could not live up to what He was asking me to do. I wanted out, because I now knew that what I had been preparing for was a fantasy and that the real desire of my heart would take obedience and sacrifice that I was not prepared to give! You know what is really funny about the fear that gripped me about being unprepared for what was starting to unfold? It was that He had not told me to do anything on the trip. He had not spoken about any new teaching or training or ministry I was to do, and yet I was totally undone over the thought of sacrifice! I would lament at the thought of quitting my cushy government job and giving up my retirement and savings. I had no idea that giving up all I knew or thought was important, would be part of the cost to see His vision fulfilled in me. To be God's man or woman will cost more than you are willing to pay. I had no way to know that He would require me to give up all our future security and the retirement I had built up. That was a bit much, and I really struggled. Most of us think of intimacy or knowing Father as a nice warm feeling and a presence that will protect us from anything difficult. Where do we get that? It certainly is not from the Word. Jesus was a rebel to the world's system. He associated with the wrong people and the "not so acceptable" crowd. He ate with sinners and publicans. Thieves and heathen always surrounded Him, or worse yet, religious fanatics who extracted the life out of people through control and manipulation. Somehow we have the attitude that Holiness, or being holy, is to live in a nice clean place, with a safe God, in a nice neighborhood. We acquaint holiness with moral cleanliness and niceness. Jesus was the holiest person ever, and He lived on the street or in other's houses, constantly traveling and being with sinners and outcasts, bringing healing and deliverance to those lost or caught in bad situations. He suffered, and constantly sacrificed His life for others even while He yet lived. The desire of my heart and the vision of God for my life were shaping up to be something other than ministry in nice churches, in fancy neighborhoods that smelled pleasant to the nose. I had prayed to know the fellowship of His suffering and the power of His resurrection in my life. I had prayed to know the love of God that passes all knowledge. I had prayed to know the depth and the height of His love toward us... OH, but this is not the way I saw Him answering those prayers... no, not, nit, absolutely not! Going back to a time before the vision was not an option, as I had spent too many years following it, and the vision was as much a part of me as breathing. Surrender is not a sweet thing, at times.

I did quit work and we did give up all our security and moved to India. In the beginning, we were helping build a training center for a ministry to the Banjara tribe (an unreached people group of India.) We also taught at a Bible school in this compound we were building, and in a few other places at different locations around India. After five months, we went to a training school in Singapore to learn how to be strategic coordinators (that is a net-worker/ resource person who works with other ministries, with a goal to reach unreached people groups of the world.) The training was strategic to us, although we did not become strategic coordinators for any unreached people group. What it did was bring together in my mind my life teaching about discipleship and intimacy. Through this thirty-day training, the Lord started to unfold to us what we were to focus on. At the end of that time, Dana went home to help her mom for a bit and I went back to India for a month. During that month I told the people we were working with that I was not sent to build buildings, but to teach and start fires for the Lord. It was a bold move, not well-received, but I did get to teach once during that time what was in my heart, and I was changed. God did several miracles and healing as He showed His confirmation to me that this is what we were to be about. There was an instant change in those leaders' lives. I went home for a month or so and then we both went back to India. From that time on, we began to share what was in our hearts and we saw the Lord move. Healings, salvations, house churches springing up, miracles happened, spiritual fires were being started, several unreached areas and people groups started to see the Lord move through the Christians in those groups and whole ministries were changed. Leaders and pastors saw the need to disciple and teach their people how to walk in close fellowship with God. So many leaders got baptized in the Holy Spirit with signs following them that it was like watching the book of Acts come back to life, only greater.

When we went back to India, what really happened was that we started being who we were created to be in Christ. It was a sudden change to those we were working with, and caused some discomfort. We scheduled a meeting of all the main pastors of the ministry we were with, about 51 of them. Dana had been with them for a financial training for two days, and then we had a day with them by ourselves to teach anything we wanted to. I had been at our home praying and seeking God while she was with them at the financial seminar. The Lord told me to teach them about Holy Spirit, and as I was praying He told me that He wanted to demonstrate His presence before I taught. When the thought that God wanted to demonstrate His presence before I began to speak entered my mind I thought, "Yeah this is just me. I want to look good, so my desire is for Jesus to show up and do a miracle to prove who I am before I teach." The thought of what He said did not leave my mind though, so I just waited, knowing if it was God, He would bring it to me as I stood up to speak. I told Dana what I thought the Lord had said and when I stood to speak, the thought that He wanted to demonstrate His presence before I began, was strong upon me. I looked around the room and my eyes settled on one man. The Lord told me to have him come up and to put my hand on his shoulder as I told the rest of them what I was going to teach on. In obedience to the thought, I did it, and as I finished talking to them about what I was going to teach on,

100

I noticed that all these pastors were looking at the man next to me whom I had my hand on. I turned, and the front of his shirt was wet with tears. He was standing there with my hand on his shoulder quietly weeping. I was impressed to ask him what had happened, and he said that he had been a pastor for 14 years and had never heard the Lord's voice, but as he stood there, the Lord had spoken to him. The Lord had told him what He wanted him to do in the future, where he would go, that He loved him and also the Lord told him he was healed! I did not know he was sick. Come to find out, he suffered with epilepsy, and that even on medication he still had some seizures.

I proceeded to teach them about Holy Spirit, and at the end of the teaching asked them how many would like to be baptized with the Spirit and Power. The denomination they were a part of did not believe in the baptism of the Spirit, yet all of them came forward and all but one received. It was a remarkable time. There was an immediate change in the ministry as these men started to see healings, deliverances and a multitude of souls saved. The Spirit of God began to move amongst the Banjara and a fire was started that burns to this day. Whole villages have come to the Lord through these men. Paul, who was healed that day, came to my house about a month later with his medications and asked if I wanted them, he said that he did not need them anymore. This last year, it has been six years since he took any meds and he is still healthy and reaching the lost for Jesus. He has seen a great many miracles as he lives out his intimacy with the Lord.

It is not enough to see God do miracles in our meetings- that is a wonderful start- but those who attend and are part of the miracles should see a change in their lives and ministry. I am not talking

101

about just "ordained" ministers here, but all who name Jesus as Lord—every believer. Most Christian discipleship meetings are in everyday life, and God's presence and miraculous power should be a part of that... like in the book of Acts, meeting daily from house to house (Acts 2:41-49.).

Jesus had started a fire in us, and almost everywhere we went and taught on intimacy/discipleship, from Baptists, to Pentecostals, the group leaders would ask me to teach them about Holy Spirit at the end of the conference/training. We saw, and still see, many Christian leaders get filled or baptized with the Spirit of God with the purpose of being a witness for Jesus. It is an amazing time.

How does this relate to intimacy or becoming God's man? All we are doing is the result of hearing and believing that we have heard from Father, and then walking it out in our lives. Our lives may look different than yours, but basically they are the same. We have things that each of us are called to, and as we walk, we share and disciple those around us into an intimate relationship with Jesus. Our destinations are tied up in our daily decisions. If we make these decisions based on what we hear and know in Jesus, and take a general direction because of what we have heard, we will end up in a place of fruitfulness and fulfillment. Dana and I hear daily, walk eternally, and live purposely. We are truly learning to trust that God is bigger than us and that He can do more that we can ask or think possible as God's children.

Kolkata,

> It is written, "Without faith it is impossible to please God." It is also written, "God has given to each man a measure of faith." From these two statements I conclude that "faith" is not our problem. (see Gal.5:6b)

We moved back to the states at the end of a year of living in India in 2001, but we (sometimes just me) took many trips to India during the next eight years. Some of those years, I was in India 7-8 months a year. One year, we were gone from home for ten months. We have also ministered in other countries, but India was the primary focus for this period of time. We learned a lot from India. About half the time Dana traveled with me, and on one such trip, while traveling around India for three months (where we stay and teach for three days in one place and then travel to a new area and another ministry continually), I had a scheduled ministry in Kolkata to a group of pastor/leaders of a non-spirit-filled denomination. We were to teach on discipleship. This was scheduled at the end of the three-month period of time and just before Christmas.

Dana was going to stay in Hyderabad, and I took one of our disciples and friends with me to do this ministry. It was on the 19th to the 21st of December. We were tired, used up, and I actually wanted to cancel this meeting. I called to do just that and was implored to come as these leaders were waiting and anticipating my coming to teach on discipleship. There were theology professors, pastors, and a graduating class of theologians at this meeting. As I remember it, there were about sixty plus people present.

In most of the meetings we do, there are lots of questions and soul searching the first day as we look at scripture and our "real" position in relationship to them as leaders. The first thing we must come to before change can happen is the revelation of where we truly are. Before we can begin to change who we are, we must realize who we are now and what we really believe. We must face what part of scriptures we actually do, and what commandments we don't do. Then we must look at man's traditions and Jesus' commands and be willing to see the truth about what we teach and walk. The first day is always uncomfortable and very challenging as we examine scripture for several hours to see the truth of our position and function. Before we can grow, we must be willing to see the truth of where we are, not where we think we are. I love the denominations that are such sticklers for scripture, because if you show them scriptural commands that they are neglecting, they will change and do what scripture says. As with all of us, the changes we need to make generally require a lot of fuss, resentment and anger at first in regards to what we have been taught. In our trainings, we work through that and then can go on to show exactly who we should be, and show how to get there. Usually during the first day or so there is a lot of frustration when we realize how short we truly fall from being exactly who Jesus says we should be. We find that most of us are very good at doing traditions, but lousy at obeying scripture commands or God's voice. As a general statement, you cannot disciple people into walking like Jesus if there is little or no intimate fellowship between yourself and Jesus. You cannot disciple someone to a place that you have no experience in, you can only take them where you have lived. This is a sad, but true statement of almost every gathering we train in; people don't live in intimacy with Father, so they cannot teach others to live there or even how to get there. These Christian brothers were no different, and the first two days were filled with wonder and frustration as we looked at a lot of scripture. By the end of two days, they realized that they needed to hear the voice of God to really obey His commands and be the men of God they desired to be. They wanted to change their priorities and some of the courses at the seminary, and there were a lot of tears and rejoicing. It was a wonderful time, and at the end of the second day of training one of the leaders came to me and asked, "Would you teach us about Holy Spirit tomorrow?" (I generally give the leaders I am teaching a choice of subjects for the last day.) I did not expect this kind of a request from this group so I told this professor I would have to check with the ministry director. When I did, I was so surprised to hear him say, "Oh, please, do teach us about the Holy Spirit and then would you show us how to receive this "baptism or filling?" In two days of going through scripture they had discovered something (that I had intentionally taught, but never spoke about), which is a need for intimate fellowship with Father, and the power of Holy Spirit to walk out Jesus' commands and desire.

I was up most of the night, praying for an open heaven and open hearts. When I arrived the next day and started to teach I was amazed at the hunger. They were not arguing with me, but these leaders were persistently asking, through their questions, for a greater understanding of what "Holy Spirit upon" was about and the power involved. We spent a lot of time going over the scriptures that last day. It took me almost four hours to get through two hours of training because they had so many questions and comments. We took no break, nor did I see many get up through this training, be-cause they were so intense and focused. The Spirit of the Lord was moving profoundly in their hearts and at the end of the time, I had them all gather in a multilayered circle. I had them confess their sin of disbelief of some scriptures and of any personal sin. Then, I had them ask for Holy Spirit to come upon them and baptize them, fill them and empower them. I began going around the circle laying my hands on each one. About the eighth one I laid my hands on was a bible student graduate whom I knew, from what the Lord had told me, had a problem with evil spirits. When I put my hand on him he made this moaning noise and bent backward at the knees until his body was at a ninety-degree angle to his lower legs. He did not fall to the ground, but his body was parallel with the floor and he was walking backward around the teaching area. Remarkably, I kept my hand on his head as he did this impossible walk, and after about three minutes he collapsed and yelled at the top of his voice some unintelligible sound. As he fell to the floor, the Spirit of God fell on the whole place. The young man just lay on the floor shaking and babbling in tongues. The others standing in the circle all started to yell, sing and shout at the same time! They were so loud that you could not tell what was being said or what they were singing. Like in Acts 2, you could only hear "this sound." "This sound" continued as I went about the circle laying my hands on each one. It continued for 45 minutes, and was so loud that the surrounding community came to the gate of this college with sticks and broke open the gate. They thought those in the compound were being murdered. There may have been a hundred or so who came into the compound and then stood and witnessed these men and women shouting and crying to the Lord in loud voices. By this time, most of them were shouting and crying in tongues! Many had stood for over an hour, at this point, with hands raised and tears flowing. As I continued to go around the area, one lady at the back of the group, of whom I could barely reach through the circle of brothers to touch her forehead with my fingers, fell over backward so hard that she broke the watch on her wrist as she hit the concrete floor she was standing on. The crowd watching this from outside the compound, surged forward as they thought that I had killed her. It took a little convincing from my friend, a native of India who was there with me, to stop them from attacking. I continued to go around the room and came to one of the main leaders of the theological college who had stood in one spot with his hands up for well over an hour now. As I approached him, I saw a pool of water at his feet and my thought was that he must have wet himself because I saw so much water on the floor. I had not given them a break and it had been close to five and a half hours now since we had begun. As I came closer to lay hands on him, I saw two tears fall, one onto each of his feet. He had stood in one spot and cried a pool of tears onto his feet. I was shocked over the picture before me of this man being lost in the Lord that long that I cried with him for a bit -- as he gazed into heaven, lost to this world.

Finally, I finished going around the place and the Spirit lifted enough for them to move from the spots they had been standing in. (All the people who had come into the compound were still there watching). These theologians and pastors then testified of what had happened. About a third of them had seen Jesus. Some had seen angels coming and going into heaven. Others had visions of their future and were told where to go and what God wanted them to do in the future. The one who had cried the pool of tears, testified that he was standing before Jesus the whole time, singing to Him in this most incredible language that he did not understand. We had been going now for almost six hours, and there was no one who wanted to leave. It was His presence that held us. After the time was finally over, I

107

was in the leader's apartment on the compound being served lunch, when the rest of the story unfolded. The leader and his wife had been doing their daily devotional two days before I came to train them (this was the day I was trying to cancel the meetings) and were in the book of Acts, chapter 2.   They began to ask themselves this question, "What if we have been wrong about the Spirit? What if there is a baptism of the Spirit?" They prayed that God would send someone to teach them and show them the Spirit. The wife also testified that while we had been downstairs having a Holy Ghost experience, she had the leaders' children with her upstairs and several of the children, along with herself, also had been baptized in the Spirit. As we were eating, they continued to cry and be in wonder at the incredible Christmas present the Lord had brought them.

Intimacy (a profound personal relationship) with God, most times, happens like in any friendship or good marriage. It takes commitment and time. As you walk, you experience the presence of the One you walk with and conversations or intimate moments are just a part of the day. They are not planned or pre-arranged most of the time. As I was trying to cancel this meeting, I knew I would not be able to because God had put in my heart that I must go.

I just wanted to rest and it was inconvenient to go, but because I have conditioned myself to follow His voice, I could not say "No." I had often wondered about the beginnings of the Church in the book of Acts -- now I knew! Experiencing Jesus meeting others' needs is such a profound teacher. Most of those men do not even know my name.

Living the Vision

> Saturate yourself in the Word and live in the anticipation of its fulfillment.

In the midst of many of these experiences with Father, I get pictures or words for people. When He shows me something or gives me a word about someone or something, many times I don't know that it is God, because it is such a subtle suggestion. To check out what I think I have heard, I will ask people questions or ask if "this that I received" is true? I need to know that I have heard from the Lord or not. I just have a thought or a word come to mind, and at times it seems so crazy. At almost every conference or training, Father will show me something about someone in the participating group. Sometimes it is a hard word like, "you are involved in pornography or you have a strong spirit of lust that is consuming your time." At times it is something gentle and soft like, "Father has felt your (specific) pain" or "your father beat you and you are always in fear of the past, but today it is broken, you are free."

I don't know how these words come, most of the time, because they are merely there inside my head. I know they are God, because who else would give them? I am seeking Father, and praying to **Him** about the meetings, so why wouldn't these words be from God? Sometimes I get impressions or pictures of something that will happen in the meetings. During the meetings I watch it come to pass; mostly I am a spectator as I watch what Father is doing. I know that these occurrences are the Lord, as I have seen the results passed on to others who pass it on to others. Why do they happen? If you spend much time with Jesus and the Father, you will touch others, and if you abide in Their presence you will be a part of what They are doing. They are about souls and destroying the works of the enemy. As you sit with people, Father will share things with you and have you touch lives around you. *As for me, I want to live continually in Their presence as They live in me. Scripture says I am seated with Jesus in the heavenlies. I am a partaker of the divine nature, a son of God, a priest and king, I am sent just like Jesus—in intimacy with Father, empowered by Holy Spirit. I am sent to free others into His presence and life. I have a responsibility to bring His kingdom and presence to bear on earth as a son of honor.*

After a few years of seeing the Lord move mightily, He told us to take a side trip and go to YWAM (Youth With A Mission) school for six months. It didn't make sense to quit what we were doing, as revival and church-planting movements seemed to follow those we worked with and everywhere we went in India. I have found that it is better to obey and trust the Father, so we turned aside. In the process of doing the YWAM training, Father taught us to understand more about serving others and Him. It was a humbling, wonderful time. O.K., so maybe not all of it was wonderful, but it was good. Actually, it was hard on us and we went through a tough time and a learning time. The Lord spoke to us in so many ways and we had so many experiences of divine intervention and miracles. The second week of our YWAM time, we went to a couple's house and they got baptized in the Spirit. After three months in Australia in a classroom environment, we returned to Hyderabad, India, to do our missionary outreach that YWAM requires. I was asked to do a church service at a small church soon after we arrived in India. As we were coming down the road to the church, a man was walking up the road. As we passed the man, the Lord told me that I was to pray for this man. When we arrived at the church this man showed up, and I laughed inside as I began to watch God unfolded His plan. I did not seek this man to pray for him, but simply went ahead with the ministry that the Lord had given me. During the service, I would hear this grunt or sound like someone was expelling air very quickly, "Uuh, uuuh" and I realized that it was the man I was to pray for. He was unable to speak anything clearly, and only one sound came from his lips. After the service was over, and we had prayed for a bunch of folks, I looked around, but this man was nowhere to be found in the building. I thought maybe I had misheard the Lord at this point, but as we went out to get our shoes (in central to Southern India, you generally take your shoes off at the door to the church) this man was not sitting **by** my shoes, but he was sitting **on** them. I started to laugh, as I laid my hand on his head, at the craziness of the whole situation. To be sitting on my shoes is so absurd; people will not touch your shoes in India, much less sit on them, because of the culture and the fact that they have no idea what you may have walked through. I had thought I missed God and was relieved the man had disappeared, and then I find him outside the building on my shoes. The instant I put my hand on him, the Lord spoke. He told me that I was to leave my hand on his head until he spoke. Holy Spirit then informed me this man spoke fluently in two languages.

Several of the men present picked the man up with my hand still on him (as the Lord had commanded me) and carried him into the church. When I had put my hand on him he had frozen up instantly. He could not move, and once in the building, after about an hour of waiting on the Lord to move through our prayers, many of those present became bored and wanted to leave. After about two hours most

111

of the people had left the room, as there was still no change in the man's condition. I continued to have my hand on his head. There had been a lot of shouting "In Jesus Name," commanding spirits to leave, and other "Christian" prayer tactics that we use when we are without guidance and don't know what to do. Nothing happened, even though much vigorous prayer had been continually spoken over him.

God had said, "Keep your hand on him until he speaks." This man was still stiff as a board and not speaking, even though we had been there several hours praying and looking for a miracle. After a while longer, I told those who were not in agreement with what we were doing, to leave. I did not ask, I told them. When it got down to about five of us, (which took almost five hours) I noticed a change in the man and simply asked him in English what his name was. He looked up at me with a smile and told me in very proper English who he was. The surprised pastor and elder immediately spoke to one another in Telegu, which is the native language in that part of India. The man I had my hand on still responded to their conversation in their language—Ha, he spoke fluently in two languages! I removed my hand and got up to leave. The pastor testified that the man had been in his church for ten years and had never spoken a single word, except grunts. This man who had been mute told us about a shaman who had put a curse on him years ago and he had not spoken since that day. Now he could speak again and was thrilled. His freedom only took about five hours, and a continuous reduction of the number of people present. I, myself, would have given up after an hour, except I had this word from the Lord that I chose not to ignore.

Many of those who left had wanted to see a miracle, but they had no perseverance to stay until what God had said came to pass. Many times we hear from the Lord, but only test what we hear, and we

112

don't stay with the "Word" we received until we see what God has said happens. That says a lot about the "Christianity" we have been taught. After ten minutes or so we grow tired of waiting, so we begin to doubt and walk away, not seeing the promise come true. If God speaks, don't quit... persevere and be patient...God is true to His word.

I have missed it at times and not heard, but thought I did. I also have thought I have not heard, and found that I had heard. Like in my marriage, my relationship with God is not perfect, nor is my hearing perfect, but as the years go by, it gets better! God does talk to his children. He wants to talk to His children.

What a Father and Lord! We are continuing to see His vision, given to me in 1983, unfold and be fulfilled. We have yet to see very many of the fires start in the Northwest, and some other countries He had spoken to me about, but we know in our hearts that God is faithful and we will see His Word fulfilled. Through this whole time I have had so many intimate encounters with my Lord and Father as I continually seek Him and His presence. I have had visions, dreams and constant encounters with His voice through moments spent with animals, ants, clouds, lightning, etc. There are so many ways that God has spoken to me, encouraged me, and corrected me. I am amazed at times when I meet Christians that as they hear me talk they will ask, "How come you are always saying God told me or God spoke to me? God does not talk to me." With each one I will spend as much time as possible showing them that God *does* talk to them. Many of these encounters with other Christians end with tears of joy as they find a new place with God, walking in a closer fellowship with Him because they know they *do* hear His voice. I am always asking others to take a risk and believe, "Why wouldn't what you hear, as you seek

Him about praying for someone, be God? Live for the audience of One, don't give up on your relationship desires, pursue Him and find the closeness with Him that is there."

What have we learned over all these years and through the good times and bad walking with Father? Three words come to mind that my Lady Dana coined at a training one time; **honor, obedience and sacrifice.** We must **honor** God and have respect and integrity in all we do with Him and His people. Sometimes honor is spelled "forgive me, I did wrong." **Obedience** is learned through sufferings and life. Without obedience we will not see the kingdom, nor will we see His vision come to pass. Choice is always the key in obedience. Rationalization is the first enemy of obedience. **Sacrifice**, not comfort, is the way of the cross. To truly walk with Jesus and have intimacy with Him we must take up our cross and follow Him. You have to die to live. If I were to sum up these three words I would say that they spell AGAPE'. You must live all three to see God's love lived out on earth in our lives. To walk like Jesus we must risk it all. Perfection has not come yet, but this we do, "We forget those things that look like failures or success and leave them behind us, and walk on toward the mark of the high calling of the Lord Jesus Christ, endeavoring to "know" Him." (A Neil paraphrase of several partial scriptures). Like David says in Ps. 17:15 "I will only be satisfied when I see His face in righteousness and awake in His likeness." Never quit or give up. Did you know that from the time that Paul was called until he truly walked in the power of the ministry God had for him, it was about 17 years? (See the book of Galations1:18 and 2:1.). I call those years the training and dying time. God knows what you must learn and when you must go. He and He alone is the One you must walk with to see your hopes and dreams come to maturity. Paul says that the

Gospel he shared was not received from man, but came by "revelation" from Jesus. Revelations are nothing more than divine communications with our Lord and Father through Holy Spirit. Paul's teachings were based on his intimate or close fellowship with the Lord. Paul had a lot of knowledge, but counted it as dung that he might attain to Jesus. _His intimacy with the Lord was more important to him than his education_. This does not mean that he forgot all he learned, what it does mean is that he put his knowledge into subjection to his relationship. He valued His relationship more than he valued position or knowledge. The word "revelation" means to take off the cover, disclose, reveal, laying bare, making naked, a disclosure of truth or instruction concerning things before unknown. This walking, in revelation based living, does not come without cost, nor without hunger and passion in one's life for " the unseen" realities of the Kingdom of God. Father gives revelations to many but to live there like Paul is another thing.

Knowing Without Reading.

> The Bible is the map of God's kingdom, but it is not "the" kingdom. Jn. 5:39

As I look back on this journey into intimacy and being discipled by the Master, God's voice is a huge part of my life. Scripture is my foundation, and even before I began reading the Word, God was teaching it to me by *talking* to me about different incidents recorded in the Word. I have found that life after God's vision began to unfold in 2000, looks a lot like life before 2000; I am just living out God's presence, doing life and continuing to "Go."

I would like to relate another's testimony that correlates the fact that God can teach someone about scripture without having a Bible to read. Since I started traveling in the Asian area, I have come across several others who have had similar experiences to the one I am about to relate. It is always interesting to meet someone who came to the Lord through the *voice* of the Lord. That is, through communicating with Jesus, the Father and Holy Spirit without a Bible, or before they read one, through experiences, vision, dreams, and words of inspiration.

I met this man from Cambodia, in the mid '80's, that had some of the same experiences I had encountered (talking to and learning from God without a Bible) only his experiences were a little more profound than mine. We were working together on an irrigation project and the wind was blowing fairly hard that day. My understanding of Jesus' willingness to work with us, in spite of our lack of a Bible, was to be enlarged. I was upwind from this Cambodian fellow about 200

116

yards, praying and singing in the Spirit, while I was putting together some parts on a circle sprinkler system we were installing. I looked up to see this man running toward me and it was evident that he was very excited. When he got to where I was, he told me that I was speaking in the same language as the man that had shown him Jesus when he was about seven years old. He said that I was the first person he had met that talked the same as that man. Because of this, he instantly trusted that I knew the same God he "knew." Over the next few days he shared his life's testimony with me and had me come to his house to meet his family. He was so excited to find someone who knew the Jesus he had met in Cambodia, all those years before. (I will call this man Khan.)

At the age of seven or so, Khan met a missionary who came to his village and taught about the name of Jesus, the cross and the blood. He remembered nothing else about that first encounter. But, as a result of this man's teachings, some of the villagers would put a red cross above their door or would put red splashes around the door to keep out evil spirits. Khan's grandmother, the witch doctor or medicine woman of the village, was always angry with these people but could not hurt them because of their belief in Jesus. As he witnessed this power that these people had over evil, Khan was impressed. You must remember that he had seen his grandma put curses on many people and had seen some die from these curses. She was much feared in other villages. When Khan was 12 or so, his grandmother was dying and it was decided that he would receive her power. He was put in a hut with her and she began to chant. As Khan watched, he could see the spirits leaving her and coming toward him and in his fear he called out on the name of Jesus. He immediately said, "Jesus, Jesus, Jesus," and as a result the demons did not come upon him.

This name was all he really knew. Khan had no Bible or training, just the things he had witnessed in others. He was run out of the village because he refused to accept the demons and be the medicine man. Years passed that he did not tell me about, but he was about twenty when the USA was involved in the war in Vietnam. Khan was a Cambodian without a family, so he was recruited by the USA to be a spy in North Vietnam. He told of being in one village that was attacked by the Viet Cong. They knew a spy was there, but not who it was. Since no one knew who the spy was and wouldn't reveal him (because they couldn't), the VC lined the people of the village up at the edge of a hole that they had dug and were shooting them down with a machine gun. When it was his turn to be in a row of people and shot, the VC who used the machine gun reloaded and test fired the gun. (It worked perfectly), but when he attempted to shoot the people in the line, it wouldn't fire. This happened three times while Khan was standing in the line softly saying, "Jesus, Jesus, Jesus." At that moment, the Americans attacked the village and everyone scattered. Khan was saved once more by simply knowing the name "Jesus."

Later, he was in another village and the VC attacked. They had found out that he was the spy they were looking for and were chasing him. They were punishing this village for harboring him. They had shot two women with children in the middle of the village, leaving the young children alive to lure people out into the open. The VC waited for someone to come and try to rescue the screaming babies and would then shoot those who came. Khan was watching and waited until a distraction happened, and then racing out, he grabbed the babies and ran away. As he fled the village with two babies in his arms, he found another lady fleeing, also with two other children. Together they traveled constantly for two days. The little ones were exhausted and they could go no further without rest and food, so Khan stopped and climbed a coconut tree to get some milk and food for the children. While they were in this clearing, eating the coconuts and resting, the VC chasing them suddenly came into the same small clearing. They could not run as they were in the open, so Khan merely sat huddling with the children and the lady and speaking softly, "Jesus, Jesus, Jesus." The VC sat right in front of them, even leaning their firearms against the tree right beside Khan and the woman and children. They did not see them! The VC made a fire and started to cook food. All of a sudden there was gunfire from the jungle, and the VC jumped up and ran off, leaving all the food they were cooking and even some canned milk. Khan and the group ate the food, then continued to run for the Cambodian border. He later married the woman and they kept the children. After they escaped to Cambodia, they petitioned to be brought to the US because of Khan being known as a spy. He received asylum and ended up being sent to the city we were then living in. All of his life he had never had a Bible that he could read. I met him in 1984, and at that time he still did not read English well. He had never shared his testimony because he had never heard anyone speak in tongues like the man that had taught in the village of his youth. During the time we shared together he was always quoting things that Jesus had told him. When Khan would speak a scripture (in his own words) I would take out my Bible and show him what he had spoken was in the Word. He said, "Surely this must be my Jesus' book, as what He `told' me is written in it." I gave him my Bible because he thought that other Bibles might read differently, for some reason. What excited me was his relating that, "Jesus had taught him," and what he had learned was scripture --- without a Bible! Much of the confusion that had come into my life,

119

with many leaders trying to tell me that the voice I had been listening to for years was not God, ended that day. I went back to trusting my conversation with God as I always had through my life, even though it came against the teaching of the church I was attending. I went back to believing what the Bible said, and I went back to my relationship of intimacy and close fellowship with God.

When you start reading the Bible, looking for a deep, close relationship with Father, you will find a lot of interesting words to confirm your quest. You will also find that from the beginning to the end of the book that this is the purpose of God— a close, dynamic relationship or "intimacy" with man. Even though the word intimacy is not found in the Bible, the concept of Father's love and Jesus' sacrifice is all about God having an intimate relationship with man; not just a casual friendship, but a deep, relational, covenantal connection with man. There are several things written in the Word that will make a difference in how or what you hear when you read the Word. The position you see yourself in with God affects *how* you hear, and your intimacy through Holy Spirit with Father and Son will affect *what* you hear.

To Know—The Importance of Hearing.

> Faith is not just a response to facts or scripture; it stems from the results of an intimate relationship through Holy Spirit and divine revelation.

I have known the voice of God for most of my life, but there is a lot of difference between Jesus as your Savior and Jesus as your Lord. Before He was Lord of my life I married and divorced twice. I did not know a thing about the Christian life, nor the commands of the Bible were. On both occasions of marriage that failed, Jesus warned me before I married, saying emphatically, "This is your choice, not mine." Then, He would tell me how long the marriage would last. But since He was only my Savior and not my Lord, I felt I did not have to obey or listen to all He said. Sometimes I was very annoyed with the fact that He could tell me what would happen before I had even told Him what I was going to do. "I disagree, you are wrong; I am going to do this my way," are a few of the statements I made when I did not want to listen to him (I was not willing to see that He knew everything in my life). I confess, I would be "at odds" and even argued with His suggestions about what He perceived I should do, more than a few times in my life.

At times, God and I have had some pretty funny conversations. I have laughed uncontrollably at some of the things He tells me. One time, I was going to speak at a Full Gospel Businessmen's convention and I was in my room getting ready for the dinner, and combing my hair (I never comb my hair). As I looked in the mirror I heard the

Lord say, "Aren't you glad that ugly is only skin deep?" I lost it, I was laughing so loud. God was giving me a hard time about primping in the mirror as if I was important or something. I put the comb down and went to the dinner.

Now, don't get me wrong, the incident was funny, but at the same time God was teaching me something. I was thinking I was someone at that moment, and the Lord used a little humor to cause me to see that I was being a wee bit vain! At times I have had the Lord tell me to watch someone as they walked into the place where I was, and as I watched, they would do something that made me laugh or at times cry. He uses life to give me what I need, and at times that is laughter. At other times it is tears. Just the other day, God started to speak to me about something that would be coming into my future and I stuck my fingers in my ears and started saying, "LA-la-la-la. I know I don't want to hear this." Yeah, I did it, and then we laughed together. Afterward, we had a good talk. Some folks have a hard time with that. I hope I am not offending anyone with the incidents I have shared, but I want you to know that life with God is about more than religious activities. He is not always serious in our conversation. Christianity is about living life with God. Fellowship is not always heavy, but fun, and filled with laughter and joy.

In the early years of my life, from the age of nine until I was thirty, I had not made Jesus **LORD**. He was my friend and savior. Jesus was my confidante, the one I talked with, and sat with. Since then, He has become Lord of my life. I have been married to one woman and we have been faithfully married for thirty-four+ years now. When I let Him become my Lord, He told me that the first two women in my life had been my choice, but that Dana was His choice. He does a lot better job of choosing than I did.

As I sit here, a scripture comes to mind, "Don't despise small be-ginnings" and this thought traverses my mind, that it is the little deci-sions that matter and that shape our future. There is something to remember in our walk with the Lord, in the fact is that He is God and you are not. Even though He is bigger than our mistakes and our thoughts (*I am not giving license here to anyone to willfully sin*). He can work through our decisions, good and bad. It is better to walk with Him and hear what He says. Father has worked through my mis-takes as I am always giving them to Him, but I would rather trust and obey than need to repent. As soon as I recognize a sin, I give it to Him to work with. I want to grow and learn of Him so all I do, good or bad, I give to Him in the hope that He can make something good out of it, in spite of me.

The thought may be coming to you; "How does he know it is God's voice and not that of another?" Good question! In answering that, here is a question back. How did Abraham know God's voice, or David, or Paul? How did these holy men of old know that they were listening to the God of all creation? The answer is simple -- He is God and His voice is a part of us.

I grew up with the voice of the Father and Jesus in my ears through Holy Spirit. I have found that **real** life is sustained by my intimacy with the Lord. As I ponder the experiences I have had train-ing leaders and Christians to listen to the voice of God, who marvel when they discover that God is talking, I wonder, "Do we read what we already believe into the Bible or believe what we read?"

You still might be asking, "How do we know it is God's voice? What if it is the devil or my own thoughts?" The answers to those questions are found in scripture and in your relationship with God. God is faith-ful to what He says is true, and we **know** God's voice; (John 10:27) -

- that is a promise! It is unfortunate that we are taught by the world and other "Christians" around us *not* to listen to Him. Everywhere in life we are taught to fear voices we hear in our head or heart. Scripture tells us that God is speaking to us, even though we have not perfected listening yet. After all these years of walking with the Lord, I still get it wrong at times, in spite of what I know. But then again, I still mess up in my relationship with my wife and what I hear her say at times, also. I misread or miss what she means. So I guess I will be O.K. with not being perfect and continue to grow in hearing what He is saying. Lady Dana and I have been together for 34+ years and are still madly in love with each other, even with all the mistakes we have made. When we miss it with each other we apologize, get up and go after our relationship again. We don't quit... it should be the same with Father.

We will never be perfect at intimacy in relationships in this world or with God. If we would really admit it, most times it is not that we don't know when God speaks - it is more simply, we just don't want to obey Him or hear what He says. You may say that is not true, but obedience to God's voice at times gets us a wee bit too close to Him for comfort. If we hear Him, we have to deal with our sins, our fears, our need for men's approval and other such nonsense that we think is important. So at times, it is safer for us to say, "That can't be God."

Even though in our heart we want intimacy, there is a price to intimacy and that is "being known"-- not merely knowing. Any good intimate relationship costs us "self" motives, and intimacy with anyone requires sacrifice. Meeting God's need for fellowship is no different. Hearing His voice will sometimes take you further than you want to go, or so you will think. God's love is worth the price and it is a safe risk, filled with wonder and joy. Step through your fear and hear from the Lord. In the midst of it all, God is speaking, but are we willing to listen?

A few years back, I was meeting with some young people and sharing with them the thoughts of hearing God's voice, personally and naturally, as He *is* our Father. I had taken them through a scriptural foundation for this intimacy I was talking about with God, and as we entered the *doing* portion of the workshop, one young lady volunteered to be prayed for by some of the others present. I selected three young ladies, about 10-12 years old, and I explained to them about hearing the Father through the Spirit while praying for someone else. I shared that Father wanted them to pray as a result of hearing from Him through Holy Spirit. John 14:26, 15:26 and John 16:8-13 talk about the Spirit teaching and guiding us into all truth so we can be His witnesses. These scriptures also say that He, the Spirit, "will show us things to come,"

I talked about how He would lead them with pictures, thoughts, words, visions or maybe even something they see with their eyes, or receive from their other physical senses. I explained to them that the first thing that came to their minds would probably be God! (Mt. 7:7-12). Why wouldn't it be God who speaks to us first if we are asking Him to lead and guide us in prayer? A good father certainly would not let a thief, robber or killer bring the answer to their children's questions before He gave them an answer. These three girls put their hands on the young lady and started to pray what they saw or heard as I encouraged them to trust that what they got would be personal and from God. They did not have to interpret what they got, but just followed the Spirit and put into words what they saw or heard. One of these girls giggled when asked what she saw or heard and she replied that it couldn't be God. I told her that it *was* the Spirit of God and that she should pray it. She would giggle more and said that it could not be God. What the other two young ladies prayed moved the young woman they were praying for, but I knew there was more. Finally, we got the other girl to tell us what the word was that she had gotten. It was the word "toes"; she had gotten clearly one word. Everyone there laughed at her word, including me, and I wondered how this was going to work. I encouraged her to start with that word and pray it, then follow with what came to her as she was speaking. When she was obedient to finally pray, she spoke, "Father, I pray over Anita's (not real name) toes." Everyone laughed more, except the young lady and myself. After a moment of silence the young girl continued, "Father, I pray that Anita would realize that You love her as much as she loves her toes. Father, I pray that she realizes that she is as beautiful to You as her toes are to her." I am watching the young woman being prayed for and she is crying. When I asked what this meant to her, she replied after a bit, that when she was young someone close to her had told her she was ugly, and it stuck with her. From that point on she thought she was ugly and she dressed accordingly, with drab-looking clothes that made her look plain. At around the same time in her life, someone had seen her manicuring her toes and remarked that she had the most beautiful toes. That statement also stuck with her, and she thought that her one good attribute was her toes. As this young girl prayed over Anita the word "toes", she knew God was talking, because no one knew about how she felt, not even her husband. This personal prayer by a twelve year old girl, who only had one word given her before she began to pray, set the young lady free and she cried in relief. Anita was a different person and her live was changed merely because a young girl was willing to hear from the Lord and pray what she heard without need-

126

ing to understand or interpret what she saw. She trusted that God would show her what to pray instead of praying general prayers with lots of scripture or words that sounded nice to the ear.

This is just one incident out of so many I have experienced as I have taught intimacy with the Father and hearing the voice of the Spirit to a variety of people and leaders around the world. Every Christian should know that God wants to talk to them and **IS** talking to them. He wants to talk to others through them. He will lead His children in prayer that breaks the root of people's problems, if they will learn to listen to what He is saying to them. Not a word that deals with just the fruit, but one that will destroy the root. Only the Spirit can do that, and we must hear if we are to represent Jesus on this earth, because we are sent just like Him!

Adding Reality to Your Relationship

> Love is not God's love unless it is given away. It is something that cannot be put into simple verbiage; it must be worn and shown. Love gives birth to faith, and faith strengthens love.

God is about intimacy and all of our teachings in Christianity must lead toward this. Jesus died to bring us back to a place of fellowship and holy, intimate communion with Father. Prayer, evangelism and then discipleship should bring people into a place of understanding their relationship with the Father and show us who we are in Christ, which will lead us to close fellowship with Holy Spirit. We tend to evangelize people into conversion and then disciple people in how to do "church" ministry and how to be "good church members," but it seems we haven't brought people into an intimate covenant relationship with our Creator. I believe that most, if not all, of ministry to the saints should be focused on bringing the whole body to an understanding that they are sons and daughters of God and to recognition of the privilege and responsibility of that position.

Tradition is the greatest threat to intimacy with God or with any close relationship. We tend to want to use our minds to create a "rule, program or method," which ends up becoming a tradition, which will set parameters to the foundational doctrine of intimacy we find in scripture. We like to establish a method or pattern of attaining something, and then teach others to do exactly as we have done. We establish procedures, thinking that will help others attain what we are trying to impart. But we must remember that we cannot actually *teach or train* someone to walk in intimate fellowship with anyone. We can impart a longing for a dynamic close relationship, but in reality intimacy can only be *found, explored, committed to,* and then *experienced.* Can there ever be a "this is the way" procedure to produce a Love relationship? Can you cut it in stone and say, "This is exactly the way you must walk to have dynamic, close fellowship?" If we were all exactly the same and reacted the same to all stimuli, maybe we could come up with a policy on intimate fellowship, but we are all as different as each star in the universe. God created us to be creators, so intimacy is itself *creative, spontaneous and unpredictable* in nature because of the variety of our life experiences and goals. It takes constant interaction and communication to maintain relationships with any depth to them. The experience is ever changing, growing or moving as our life experiences take us to *new choices, spiritual planes and emotional thresholds.*

Can you imagine having the exact same words each morning spoken with the same tones, at the same time, with your loved ones for ten years? I think that they would grow to hate those words, because they would realize that they had no meaning. They would recognize that these words are only a part of your daily routine. Why would we think that God is different in this? Do you think that He might get bored with our religious practices that we do each day? Do you think that God likes repetition or does He like spontaneous creativity in His relationship with man? Think about this; "Why is every sunset different, every wave of the sea different, every snowflake unique and every person one of a kind?" I believe Father wants freshness each day in His relationship with man. He loves our creativity and passion to be used in our relationship with Him. It brings a reality to the words of love that we speak with our mouths.

When Dana and I got married, she had been abused in various ways by several people. Her family was dysfunctional, like so many others, and her mother had been an angry lady. There was sexual abuse by men in her past, and she was not a fully functional person in many areas of her life. How could she be-- intimacy to her meant pain? For her, love was not defined with joy, and "I love you" meant, "I want to manipulate you, use you, or abuse you in some way." My perspective of love was not much of a help to her, since I thought that love was doing something nice to someone else (like my wife) for the sole purpose of getting what I wanted. My perspective was all about "self." Somehow, in my fractured past, I had never learned about true love either. What I had seen of love had nothing to do with the God kind of love. My mother and father had never kissed or hugged in my presence. The only time I had seen them kiss was on their 25th wedding anniversary. My dad never hugged me, which I can remember. This sterile concept of love did not help Dana or our marriage. Not long after we were married I wanted Dana out of my life, as she was not "giving me what I deserved." I was so selfish and filled with arrogance that eventually I wore her down, and she tired of my selfishness. She left to go to her mother's for some time away. I had to make her want to leave so I could say the marriage failure was *her* fault. Most men hate being the ones who are the reasons for anything failing and we will constantly try to make some sort of ra-tionalization so that failure is not our problem. I wrote her a letter while she was gone, and told her pretty clearly that I did not think much of her. (Remember me saying that God had said that she was His choice? Well, I was not going for it). Then, on the day she was to come home from her mother's, I left this letter for her to read upon arrival. I knew what I had written would cause her to pack up and leave.

Something funny happened around noon that day; God started talking to me. Even though I can't say I remember any actual words coming from Him, He began to impress on my soul that without Dana I would be nothing. I was filled with fear that she would leave and I would die as a result. I realized that I did not want to live without her. I needed her, and I had never needed anyone! This was a complete surprise to me, so I rushed home hoping to get to the letter before she read it. As I pulled into the driveway I realized I was too late, because her car was in the yard, and I was undone. I went into the house and found her sitting at the table with the letter in her lap. She was devastated. I begged and pleaded with her to give me one more chance to prove I loved her and that the letter I had written was a lie. She finally consented to give me two weeks to prove my love to her. I would live and sleep in one room, and she and my son would live in another. She told me very pointedly that even I knew I could not prove my love to her in two weeks. I had no idea how to love and I had no hope of being able to get her to stay after two weeks. She told me to go back to work and leave her alone after I had torn the letter up and threw it away. I left as a broken man. I stepped out the door and talked to the only One I knew who could help -- Jesus, my friend (but not Lord) and He was there waiting. I asked Him to help me love Dana. I did not know how to do that, so I asked him to teach me to love her the way she needed to be loved and not the way I wanted to do it. **That was the greatest prayer I have ever prayed**, and in just three days we were back together. I have never looked back. I am so in love with that woman still! I am so amazed that she would stay with me and that she actually loves me.

God loves intimacy! God showed me how to prove that I loved and needed her (although I still have my moments of stupidity or of mis-hearing or reacting wrongly to things she does or says). Dana and I have learned through the years, that for intimacy and friendship to grow, we individually must be concerned about the other's needs more than our own. We have not perfected this, but we are still learning how to love each other more like Father loves us. It is inter-esting, because in our growing love experience, Jesus is not just teaching us to love one another the way that we each need to be loved, but He is also teaching and showing us how He loves the world. We have learned that true intimate fellowship requires those three little words to be present in our love daily; **honor** for each other, **obedience** to our commitment to love and **sacrifice** to show the depth of our love.

Unity, Community and Choice

> God tells us that what we sow, we reap; not what He sows we reap. Our choices create the intimacy, or lack of it, that we live in with each other and with God.

God is a God of unity, community, and love -- not of separation, loneliness and fear. Choices will and do create our future. What have your choices created today, and what will they create for you tomorrow?

One day a few years back, before Dana and I started doing ministry around the world, I was having a conversation with my Friend and Father while I was driving into town. I was remarking about how I should have this and that and it was not fair that my friends were doing more and receiving more (temporal) blessings than I was, even though we started sharing the Gospel at the same times. I was possibly complaining. The Lord and I were talking and sharing with each other that day and the conversation came around to obedience and disobedience to some of the things He had asked me to do, and "My choices."

It is amazing to me how one can start a totally innocent conversation with Father and it end up being something that one really did **not** want to talk about. I had started the conversation talking about a possible negligence on His part with us, and it ends up being a conversation about "my choices." After a few "excuses" on my part, the Lord spoke very clearly to me, "I will show you what your choices have cost you, Me, and My Kingdom."

In a flash, He started showing me decisions I had made where I did not do what He had asked me to, and then He showed me times when I had chosen my wife's word over His, along with times I had shared more than He had spoken and what the results had been. He proceeded to let me see people who had been destroyed because I had not gone to see them when HE had asked me to go. My excuses many times were either, "I am just too tired today, or I don't think I can do that." As He was sharing these moments with me, there was one thing that came to mind; that God does not always have some-one else to send. You may be the last one to be sent before tragedy strikes, or the only one that someone else will listen to. As God was sharing these moments about my choices, I realized things I did not want to know.

After God had shown me the costs to Him, others, and myself for some of my disobediences, I was broken in an instant and having a hard time getting the car I was driving stopped and off the road without crashing. I was overwhelmed with the results of my deci-sions, my CHOICES! I had created life at times and death other times. I cannot tell you how worthless I felt. Interestingly, He was not condemning me, but instead He was showing me, convicting me, and loving me with the Truth.

I had never really wanted to consider the fact that "my choices" have that much impact on my own world, much less in His. _I don't want people to be paranoid about choices_ yet the fact remains that our choices do create different futures, for not just us, but in a much larger sense- others' lives and God's kingdom. Our choices affect our relationships and the intimate communications involved in them affect the future.

Since that discussion with the Father I have made some changes about how I make choices, and I take making decisions much more seriously. I still struggle and make mistakes, but I think that life is better and I make fewer wrong moves because I am listening and I understand a little more about creation and man's part in it. If I am *sent* "like" Jesus then I can *hear* from Father and be *led* by the Spirit as He was when He was on earth. I have not just the right, but the responsibility to hear and know His will and ways and I can be directed on earth as He was. Choices are much simpler when you have a Father you can trust, who will lead you and guide you through Holy Spirit. He knows what could be coming into your life, depending on your choices, and would guide you to right choices if you allow Him to, because He knows the end from the beginning.

I only have one real choice to make... to trust or not to trust Him. The rest of the choices change with that one- the one that receives His guidance. It sounds like a simple thing, but as we know in this world... it is not always easy. Fears, peer pressure, needs, lack of intimate fellowship and many other "things of this world" would like topersuade us not to trust, listen or obey Him. He made everything that exists; He knows the future and the past. Maybe the following question should be in our hearts constantly; *Which is more dangerous; to trust and obey Him or to trust and obey our fears or the pressures of the world that cause us to doubt or disobey Him?*

The choice is really ours, and our choice will change the world and His Kingdom!

Prayer, Listening and Burn Testimony

> Prayer is not a part of the Christian walk; it *is* the Christian walk.
>
> Prayer is a two-way connection, not a one way conversation.

Our prayer, and the way we pray, displays to others our true relationship with Father. Prayer is the communication that exhibits our true relationship with Father. If Father lives in us and we are sent like Jesus, His voice, visions, dreams, words, and the other forms of talking that God uses, should be thought normal, not special. Christians are so afraid of hearing voices or seeing pictures when they pray, that they miss having intimacy with Father, as I have stated before.

Prayer could be called the language of communion or intimacy with Father. With that thought, what is it about prayer that tends to lend itself to traditions or formulas so often? Many times our substitution of form for communion says something about our relationship, don't you think? We tend to assume that prayer is some holy posture or petition rather than it being a communion of intimacy. Our definition of prayer has to do with the depictions we see in pictures, movies, and books of Christ's life on the earth. A great portion of our definition of prayer comes from the religious practices we see in church. We are to hold God in reverence and awe, but we need to stop making intimacy with the Lord so mystical or out of reach for the normal Christian or real person.

We see in scripture that God says if we ask Him for something we should expect Him to answer with good things. Our definition of *good* may have to change because our thoughts are mostly temporal or from the viewpoint of our fleshly desires, and are not from God's perspective. Good has to do with bringing us closer to God, and evil has to do with what will cause death or separation from God. I believe that God knew that the Body of Christ would come to a place where we mistrusted voices and relationships.

We really have no expectation of hearing an answer when we pray because it has been taught out of us. There are so many scriptures which state that when we pray we will hear or get an answer. Yet we teach by our actions and attitudes that God doesn't really answer all prayers or that we don't need to know the answer, we simply need to trust God. There are prayers we pray that we don't really need to know the answer to and we do need to trust Father; yet even in these, Father will speak to us and tell us that we need to trust Him and not worry about it.

Why wouldn't what we hear or see when we pray be some kind of answer from God, after praying to God? Our actual answer or the fulfillment of the prayer request we pray may take awhile to come, but God answers or speaks to us when we ask Him, just like a father would answer a child when asked a question.

As an example; many years ago we were financially challenged to the point that we would have only $5 left over from our paycheck for anything in the range of entertainment or extras of any kind. Jon, our son, asked us one day if he could please have an ice cream treat when the ice cream man came into the neighborhood. He had no idea about our financial situation and to tell him would leave him confused and worried. If my son asks for some ice cream, even though I may not have the money for ice cream right then, I would answer and tell him, "I can't afford the ice cream right now. When I get paid we will get some." I would not just turn and walk away from him and ignore his question. God is a better father than I am and He answers us even if we can't have what we are asking for right then. He talks to us like a father would and should. He does not give us the silent treatment very often, except when He has spoken to us and we refuse to hear. The answer we gave to Jon did not please him, since we said he would have to wait, but he was so thrilled when we surprised him with a box of fudge sickles that all of his disappointment was forgotten.

It would be nice if we would accept the Word as it is written, and not make excuses about what isn't happening. We need to judge our lives by the Word, and not the Word by our lives. If we come up short of what it says should be our lives, we need to not condemn ourselves, but ask God to show us how to change our position so we can see the truth written in the Word. We need to find the truth and change so that what we see lines up with what is written. The Word won't change, but we can, and should. (What you "believe" or what I "believe" won't change the truth, but when we accept the truth, it will change us!)

When I pray I need to expect to hear from the Lord, if I really have any type of relationship at all with Him. He will answer or He is a liar. And since we know He is not a liar, we need to learn how to hear, or find a way to recognize His answers. He is true to His Word and we need to have confidence in Him and our relationship with Him. We need to know He is talking or will answer and then be willing to see or hear the answer.

In listening for God, we need to take off the restrictions of how He can speak to us. All communication is not found in only our speaking. Actually only about 10-20% of what we say is found in our words, according to the experts. Non-verbal communications are a lot higher percentage of our conversations than our words. We are created in God's image, so do you suppose that God could speak to us without saying a single word also? I think He does, and I believe scripture supports this because God has spoken to so many with pictures, situations, destitution, prosperity, nature, etc. Picture this; a large rock precariously balanced on the face of a cliff moving ever so slightly in the wind. Without a single word that rock speaks! How about this; a lush green patch of vegetation in the middle of the desert? This scene, or even the thought of it, brings a vision of rest or rescue from a harsh time or environment, or a thought of having your thirst satisfied. You understand without a single word being spoken.

I believe that we Christians would change the world if we actually heard from God all He is speaking. Hearing God, and acting on *what* we hear, might make the world a little more interested in what and who Jesus is. We need a reality-based relationship with Jesus. The Word, as the "concept" of Jesus, will not change the world. Only a reality-based Christianity will work in this post-modern era we live in. Prayer should change things and not leave the environment or people the same. God's kingdom is the reality of Christ's presence in you, exposed to all and in all you go through.

One day, in the early '80's, on the way to work, I was quite troubled by my lack of being able to pray without ceasing. No matter how hard I tried, I could not maintain prayer at all times. This troubled me to the point of frustration, as I wanted to please my Father so much. I desired to know Him and to trust Him, and that day He answered my frustrated request with a question. I was talking to Him about how to pray without ceasing and confessing my inability to do this when He came back with a simple question, "What if your interpretation of 'prayer' is wrong?" After a moment, He added, "What if prayer was simply keeping your heart open to me at all times -- could you do that?" There was an instant peace that settled in my heart. I **could** do that. The tears of anguish changed to tears of joy because I could be open to Father while doing other things. Prayer without ceasing became possible in an instant when He spoke, and my whole life changed. My prayers changed, and my living changed, because I could stay in touch with my Father at all times! It is like calling someone on the phone and then just staying on the line forever. I don't hang up, but I stay on the line and tuned in for further instructions and conversation from above. My definition of prayer was changed forever. Prayer is not just talking, but also has to do with listening and being aware of the other party's communication. It is an intimacy of communion with our Father in heaven with all the senses involved. The scriptures that said that Jesus, the Father, and I would be One (Jn. 17:20-23) took on new meaning. To be in constant communion could change everything.

There are a lot of scriptures about hearing His voice and knowing His voice that should affect our prayers. Many of these can be found in John 10, and I have found that being in the attitude of listening, without preconceptions, makes hearing much easier. Many of us listen with a preconceived notion of what, how or when God will speak. We need to simply listen and expect Him to speak, because hearing the truth leads to freedom and more than we can really comprehend. It leads to being Jesus' presence to others. When you are in His presence, you can minister and share from a different place, a place of

Spirit and Power. When we start to trade in our traditions for what the Word actually says, we will find a difference in our Christianity. I want to be a demonstration of truly being filled with His Spirit and power. To do that, I will have to continue to change and see that what we have considered church may not be even a resemblance of what the Church *should* look like. We have been searching for a reality-based experience like the book of Acts shows us, and one of the main hindrances of our finding what we are looking for is our view of what prayer really looks like. We want Acts 2 to happen and come alive in our lives, but we need to look at Acts 1 first.

One day, shortly after I had my revelation on prayer without ceasing, I was on my way to work as an electrician for a corporate farm in Nampa, Idaho, and the Spirit moved me to pray *to be used* that day. I had not seen someone come to the Lord through my life or testimony for about a month, and that was a long dry spell for me. As I was responding to the Father, I cried out, "Whatever it takes, Lord, use my life today. Even if I must die or lose an arm to see someone saved, Lord, use me! My life is yours." I should not have to tell you what an illworded prayer that was! The result of that prayer is a remarkable story.

When I got to work that day, my boss met me and asked if on my way home that evening I could stop at another of his ventures and test an irrigation pump to see if it was safe to use. Each year in the springtime, before you turn on the water for your crops, you test the equipment to make sure it is in a usable and safe condition. What he wanted was for me to check out and test the irrigation pump before use. When I got to the irrigation pond, the farm manager was there and I proceeded to test the 480 volt 100hp pump. I bypassed a few controls to start the motor momentarily, without water being in the pond, and then pushed the button. The panel, which was three foot high by two foot wide, blew up and shot flames 15 ft. across the control room. My arm and the side of my face and body was about 1 ft. from the panel. The resulting burns covered about 11-15% of my body. My arm and hand were burned with deep 2nd and 3rd degree burns. As I was slapping myself to put out the flames on my body and arm, I was amazed to hear myself saying, "I give this to You, Jesus. I surrender this to you, Lord. Use this for Your glory!" I was astounded that I was saying these things, as it made no sense. The manager took me to the hospital and a plane was eventually arranged to transport me to a regional burn center in Salt Lake City, Utah.

I could not get away from the thought that God had a purpose in allowing this to happen to me, and I remembered my prayer that morning about His using me regardless of the cost. I found myself at peace in the midst of all the pain and turmoil, as I was sure that God had a plan, even though this did not really fit into my realm of thinking, "God use me!" In the emergency room at the hospital, I could hear the emergency radios of various ambulances and police bands, and as I was laying there waiting for the plane to take me to the regional burn center, a call came in about two men being burned over 60 to 80 % of their bodies. There had been an explosion at a mill in Riggins, Idaho, and these two men had been covered with burning industrial oil. I knew that this was what God was working on and somehow knew that one or both of these men were to be saved, because the plane that was coming for me could take these men to the burn center instead of my going. I could wait, as I knew I would be O.K. God had worked it out so that the plane was already in route and that would save a lot of time in getting them the life saving care

142

they needed. God was talking and revealing His plan, so I asked my pastor of the church we were attending that was at the hospital with me, "Please pray that these men will make it out of the mountains and to the hospital in time to take my plane, I can wait for another one." The pastor informed me that I was not thinking clearly and that I needed to take that plane and that these men could wait for another one. He told me that they were not my responsibility. At that point, I asked that man to leave my hospital space and go away, and then I prayed the prayer which asked for God to save *them*!

There were several things going on at that time that I did not know about. One, was that even though the Burn Center had two planes that carried burn victims from remote locations to the hospital, one was broke down and the other one was the one coming for me. NO other plane would be coming for those men, and no other plane was available to take me.

The men did make it out of the mountains in time, and were in a hospital in Boise, Idaho, a city close by where I was located, and the plane that was sent for me was sent to get them. One of the burned men elected to stay in the city hospital that he was in and he died that night, while the other man took the plane sent for me back to the burn center. When the plane landed it had an instrument malfunction, and it was eight hours later before it was repaired and finally came back to pick me up. If I had taken that plane, the badly burned man would not have made it to the hospital for at least another eight hours and would have probably died also. When I arrived at the hospital, the doctor, who had been working on this man who took my plane the night before, was lying asleep on the bed I was to be put in. He had worked all night to keep this other man alive. This sawmill worker was burned over 60 % of his body. When I asked the

143

doctor how he was doing, I was told bluntly that, "He is burned over 60% of his body and we believe his throat is burned, he will be dead in three days". I was so full of drugs for the pain and also basking in the joy of knowing God was at work, I said very boldly, "We will see!" The look on the doctor's face and the nurses in the room was incredulous, and I wish I could have gotten a photo of their expression as I said, "We will see." I know they thought I was really out of it, but I had heard from God, and in three days instead of being dead, this guy was not only alive, but was up walking!

In 1983, when you had burns like mine, one of the treatments was an iodine bath once a day for the affected areas. My arm and hand were the major area of burns, so I would be required to put my arm in a pan of iodine water each day and scrub the affected area (the whole arm) with a wire brush. My arm was not a problem, as it was 3rd degree burns and the nerves were burned deeply enough I had no feeling. It was just a process of scrubbing the area with a brush designed to safely slough off the dead tissue. My hand was different, though, and it was extremely painful as it still had nerves that were functioning and they were exposed to the iodine, so cleaning it was a bit painful, to say the least. When I would come in to have my "iodine bath," I would stick my arm in the water with no fear of pain, as there was no feeling, until the fifth day. Dana was not with me, but was at home still arranging things for the boys so she could come and be with me. She had been at a women's retreat when I was burned, and it is quite a story in itself to hear all she went through in the first few days after the accident. There was so much going on, and God saw us both through it, but it was hard times. On the foruth night, my wife's friend had called the 700 Club and had them pray for me, and also our church had a prayer time for me. That night, I slept

144

for the first time since the incident for more than two hours, so I was refreshed and ready for my bath that morning, but when my arm went into that iodine water, I thought I would die. I had done just like all the other days, and had quickly immersed my arm into the treated water. I did not know that kind of extreme pain existed! They say that pain is good when you are burned because it means there are nerves that are alive, but at that point I was quite sure that they were wrong, because all I could do was cry and scream. The nerves had been dead, and now they were alive! The nurse and therapist came running in to see what was going on, and both were amazed at the pain I was going through. After they got me to quiet down and tell them what was going on, one of them looked at the arm and said, "I think there is skin growing on this arm, but that is not possible."They had pictures of the arm from the first day and got them to look at, and then looked closely at my arm as it presently appeared and stated that something strange was going on. All I knew was that where there was no pain, there was now!

Dana came that day, and I wish I could say that I was who she needed me to be at that time. But I was in such pain that I reacted to everyone with anger, even my Lady Dana. She was so amazing because she took it all and came through it still loving me, in spite of my attitudes. It was not a good time, as we both were reacting to the pain in the other. She had an amazing strength, and I think that if it had not been for her, I would not have made it through the ordeal.

On Friday, the doctor came in to prepare a group of us for skin grafts on the Monday following, and when he got to me he stated, "I am not going to operate on this arm, there is skin growing on it." Halleluiah! On the day that they were going to operate and perform skin grafts, I went home with my wife - eight days after the incident.

The man who was burned so badly was still alive, against all odds, and during the days I was in the hospital I watched this man get up and walk every day. He showed such fortitude, as did many of the patients there with severe burns. This mill worker was special because every nurse and doctor knew he should be dead. He was not in very good shape, with lots of reconstruction and pain lying ahead of him, but he was a fighter.

The doctor had said to me that I would never work again as an electrician, and even though I was no longer going to have surgery, he gave me no chance of being able to return to life as I knew it before the accident. My hand would not close completely, and my arm could not be bent. I had so little movement in the arm and hand that it was basically useless for any type of task, but something in me never gave up and I was determined to be whole. I had a promise from God, and I was always fighting for more movement in my arm because of that promise. Fighting for a promise of God in the physical is different than fighting from a promise given by the Spirit. I was constantly aware that God was doing something, but I was totally focused on returning to my normal life and not a happy camper because of the challenges and the pain involved to get there. I did not understand why it was taking so long for me to be healed. He was my healer. In the midst of this time He had gotten it across to me that I was going to be healed. He had restored skin and feeling, but there was not a lot of movement as there was still some very heavy scarring. Regularly I had to go back to the burn center and be examined. Each time the doctors would remark about how my having feeling and new skin were impossible, yet I had limited movement in my arm and I could not grip anything tightly with my hand. They said I was "strange." I began to be able to move more and have more

146

flexibility in my arm and hand. Some little spots of fresh skin that appeared were the key, but why were they there? Because God is good! I was thrilled that after five weeks I could move my arm enough that when I really tried, I could eat with my left hand again. It was a real chore, but I could do it. I am left-handed, and the burn was on the left arm... so this was wonderful to be able to feed myself! At five weeks, I went back to work. It was hard because I had to compensate for a loss of movement in my left arm and the grip of my hand. I found some innovating ways to do that and was relieved to be able to do something constructive. I hate sitting around and being helpless!

The doctors were amazed when I told them I was back to work. They said that was impossible. Each time I went to the hospital for checkups, I would go to the burn ward and see how the sawmill guy was doing. He still did not know about my prayer or what transpired the day of his accident.

Eight weeks after getting burned, I was sent to California to work on an irrigation machine there in the desert. My arm was not healed yet, even though there was fresh skin in places and I had some movement in it. There was still a lot of fresh scarring. In the extreme desert heat these areas became dry and cracked and were bleeding all the time. There was a lot of pain and frustration in me as I could not do physical work, but had to show others how to do my work and then stand around in the heat and watch. I was angry at God and at the burns and tired of hurting and being in severe pain. Isn't it crazy how we start to blame Father when we become frustrated or in pain? Nothing I did helped change what was going on with my arm, so in desperation I called on my Friend for some answers, one more time.

On Wednesday, on the way back from the desert to the hotel, I cried out. I told Him I would go to a church that night and I needed to hear from Him. When I got to my room, I opened the phone book and simply stuck my finger on a church name. I called the church and was informed that they did not have Wednesday night services, but instead had small groups. This just added to my frustration and I was relaying that feeling to the fellow on the phone. The man heard my desperation and said, "I am the assistant pastor of our church. Why don't you come to my college group? You can get some fellowship there and have a good time." I conceded out of desperation, and went to his meeting. When I arrived, there was a person who was sick and blowing their nose into a tissue, who was the greeter at the door. There were about twelve young people there. One had a broken leg, one had an arm bandaged up, several were sick with some kind of flu or cold and one had a sprained wrist. I was thinking, "Man these guys are in worse shape than me." The pastor finally arrived, and after introducing himself to me says, "Let's pray." I was watching the group as he was praying. I was looking around checking out what the others were doing. In the midst of his prayer, he stopped, looked up, and began to speak to me personally. Have you ever seen those shows where the action freezes, like on "<u>The Matrix</u>," where everyone is frozen in the midst of movement? Well, that is what happened. It was like everyone froze, and there was no movement. One man was holding a cup of coffee half way raised to drink when God began to address me through this pastor. "I told you that I would heal you! I brought you out of the fire and you have movement in your arm. I spoke to your heart and said I would take care of this... I want you to stop complaining, I have healed you!" There were some other words, but for the most part those are the ones that stuck to me. I was

floored! Wow, God was speaking through this man and I was undone! I apologized to Father for not listening and trusting Him and
what He had told me while I was in the hospital. The man went back
to his prayer to open the meeting, and people started to move again,
then He closed his prayer. I was broken and at the same time in
peace. This pastor proceeded to pick up his Bible and start to share
about what the message was to be that night. His subject was -- *Why
God does not heal anymore...*, and that was what he proceeded to
share on. He talked about how we have doctors now and God does
not heal like He used to in early Bible times. I was sitting there in
awe, because God had just chastened me through this man and told
me I was healed. Now this pastor was talking about why God does
not heal anymore! I left and went back to my room, contemplating
what had just taken place. The next day I got up with no cracks in
my arm, no bleeding, no pain, and new skin in places that were nothing but scars the night before. The whole arm did not look healed
and to this day some scars remain. But I have complete movement
and hair even grows on most of it. The healing progressed rapidly
from that day with a tiny patch of new baby skin at the inside of the
elbow. In every place that I needed to have movement, new skin
showed. The elbow, wrist, the back of my hand, my fingers, all those
necessary areas started to change and in the process of about three
days I had almost complete movement in my arm and hand.

On the way home, I had to stop for my final check up at burn center. When I got there in the waiting room, there was a man with an
artificial left arm and I asked him what had happened. I was sitting
there flexing my left arm and hand as he relayed a story to me about
how He had done **exactly** the same thing that I had done and lost
his arm. He was working on the same size motor and panel type that

I had been working on, checking it before the farm began to use it in the spring for irrigation. He had bypassed the same controls I had and then when he started the motor, the panel blew up. Everything was exactly the same as I had done! There was one difference, he had no arm, and I had complete use of mine. I sat and wondered at the grace of God and was moved to tears as I waited for the doctor to check me out. I could not tell the man with the artificial arm my story. At that moment how could I explain why I was healed, and he was not? I did not have the words to express what I was feeling. It is a bit disconcerting to have Father show you His grace while right next to you someone is living without it, for some reason beyond comprehension. As the doctors were checking me out and looking at the new skin on my arm, they marveled at what good grafts they had done. I instantly and vehemently corrected them and stated that they had done nothing to my arm, and that what appeared to be grafts was new skin from God. They got the pictures and my file out and conceded that they had not touched my arm. They were amazed and perplexed as they looked at the fresh skin and watched me move my hand and arm. There was no explanation for it other than God. The only thing they could say was, "You are weird." I can live with that.

I felt prompted by the Spirit to go see the man who had taken my plane in the beginning of this incident and who was alive in spite of what the doctors said would happen. As I got to the floor of the burn ward, his wife, whom I had met once before I left the hospital, was in the hallway outside the burn ward. When she looked up and saw me, she ran and fell into my arms sobbing. I did not really know this lady, yet she was falling apart in my arms. She looked up at me while still in my arms and cried with anguish, "My husband quit moving two days ago, he gave up. The doctors say if he does not start to move

150

again soon, the toxins will build up in his system and he will die. What do I do?" I had never told him or her, or the doctors about my prayer the day of the incident, nor about the plane and all that had happened. God prompted me to tell them all that day. When I entered his room, his wife sat across the bed from me, next to him, close to his head, like me.

You must realize this man has no ears, no nose, no eyebrows and no lips. He has been **very** badly burned. It was hard to sit next to this man who had suffered so much loss without breaking down into tears. I proceeded to tell about my prayer, the plane, what the doctor said when I arrived, and what God had gone through to save him. As I was talking, I noticed that the whole room had filled up as I was giving the testimony of what God had done for him. The doctor, therapists, nurses, and patients were all confirming my story to him. Heads would nod when I would make a statement, and affirmations were made about times and events. When I finished, I said quietly, with tears brimming my eyes, "How dare you give up, how dare you quit after all God has done!" I was watching his face and on the cheek next to me, a tear welled up and started to slide down the leathery skin of his face. My hand was on his shoulder, under that cheek, and that tear dropped onto my hand. He then turned to his wife and said, "Honey, can you help me get up? I think I want to go for a walk." The tears that filled that room were awe-inspiring. As I got up to leave, this man who had quit and was ready to die, was now getting out of his bed to live! I was moved deeply by the tear on my hand and the grace of God upon him. A few months later, I was giving my testimony somewhere in Idaho, and a man attending the meeting happened to live in the same town as the burned mill worker. He wanted to check out my story, so he went to his house to find out if what I was telling was true. I got a call from him after he had visited the burned man and he conveyed that one more man had given his heart to the Lord that day. I have never seen the burned man since the day in the hospital all those years ago, but God had answered the prayer that I had prayed that particular morning, "Use me Lord! Whatever the cost, let my life be the reason for someone being saved today." There is so much I do not understand about this incident to this day, but this I know; God is good, and He takes our vows to Him seriously!

Through the whole process, even though it was very hard and caused a lot of turmoil in my family and in my life, God was speaking. I cannot say I never had doubt, because at times I felt totally without hope and I was frustrated and did not understand what was happening. I was mad, at times, but God was talking to me through it all, and when I needed to hear, He spoke. Whenever I needed to be assured of His word, He would speak to me in a way that I would understand. I can tell you that His ways are not my ways. I learned a lot about trust and prayer though those months and I got a lot of lessons on intimacy. Once more I could say I was being discipled by the Master.

The Foolishness of Listening and Obeying..

> Obedience to a loving God is the only sign we can give that shows we actually trust Him.

Through the years of walking with the Lord, endeavoring to listen more and talk less, one fact continuously surfaces. The foolishness of God and man's constant rationalization of what God says to him.

1 Corinthians 1:26 – 1:31 (NKJV) [26]For you see your calling, brethren, that not many wise according to the flesh, not many mighty, not many noble, *are called.* [27]But God has chosen the foolish things of the world to put to shame the wise, and God has chosen the weak things of the world to put to shame the things which are mighty; [28]and the base things of the world and the things which are despised God has chosen, and the things which are not, to bring to nothing the things that are, [29]that no flesh should glory in His presence. [30]But of Him you are in Christ Jesus, who became for us wisdom from God—and righteousness and sanctification and redemption— [31]that, as it is written, *"He who glories, let him glory in the LORD."*

Have you ever thought about God's foolishness? "Abram, leave your family and go to a land I will give you." All Abram had was just a voice in his ear. With Moses, He used a rod to part a sea and at one time to become a serpent that swallowed other serpents. Moses also had a burning bush which was not consumed, talk to him. Joshua was told to walk around a city for seven days and blow a few trumpets and the very thick city wall fell down. Jesus spit on some road crud and anointed a man's eyes with it for healing. He simply spoke a word to a Samaritan lady about her love life and she brings a whole village to hear Jesus. Peter saw a vision that caused him to visit a person of a different culture that, as a Jew, he would never have gone to without the vision and understanding (Peter and Cornelius.). Ananias heard a voice telling him to go see a man who had Christians killed or imprisoned, and he went! He had no scripture to follow, only the voice of God.

One time a farmer came into this church in Mountain Home, Idaho, where we attended and where we were seeing lots of crazy, God stuff happen. The whole bunch of us in that church were crazy for the Lord. Most of us had lived wild and unbridled in the world, and were just as wild for Jesus. My pastor friend and I were in the church office one day, when this farmer came in asking, "Can you help me?" I was not sure what he was going to ask, but my answer was, "Sure!" It turned out that he had a crop of sugar beets that were worthless. Growing season was over, and harvest time was here, and when he took the test loads of the crop from his field to the buyers, the beets tested were of no value. The test report in his hand said the beets were worthless. As I remember it, this man was the third generation to own this farm and he was going to lose it because the hail had ruined his wheat crop and now his sugar beet crop was no good. At this point in his meandering story, I felt that I may have stepped over the line with my telling this farmer that we could make a difference.

Soon we were following this farmer out to his field in the pastor's car and my friend asked me, "What are you going to say when nothing happens with this man's crop?" Somewhere in me God was speaking, but I had no words to answer. (I don't have to try to have faith or work something up that will look good to others). I knew God was going to change this crop, what I did not know was how He was going to do it! When we arrived at the field, we got out and were standing next to the farmer's truck when I saw an old can of used engine oil in the back of it. I knew at that moment we were to anoint his crop with this "engine" oil. We proceeded to go to all four corners of his field and anoint the land with used engine oil. Then, the pastor and I spoke over the crop and said something like, "Let this be the best crop he has ever harvested!" In about 10 minutes we were done. The farmer looked at us as we were getting in the car, as if to say, "Is that all you are going to do?" I think he expected some more holy rituals or more religious words—anything probably would have helped him feel better about what we had done. I had nothing more that I felt to do, so we got in our car to leave. The farmer yelled, "Wait, what do I do now?" He was leaning in the pastor's window and my pastor friend moved his head back out of the way and both he and the farmer were looking at me, anticipating some very valid answer, it seemed. I told them, "It is Friday, so on Monday, dig some new test loads and take them in and have them graded again." My pastor friend thought I had lost it, but went along with what I had said, and then we left. On the ride home, you could have heard a pin drop in that car. It was not our most unified moment, but the friction between us soon was dropped in light of what the Lord was doing at the meetings we were a part of. Tuesday, the following week, the farmer brought a new test report to us. The report stated that the beets were excellent quality and it was the best crop he had ever raised! God is so good! I am not sure who was the most surprised, him or us. It was quite a day! God had changed a crop that was worthless, into the best crop he had ever harvested in his lifetime, in three days.

What I did was foolish, but I didn't even think about it until it was over. That is the way it is with me. I do not think about what the Spirit tells me to do at the time; I simply respond and usually put myself out on a limb, hoping I have heard. In this case, after the crop was changed, I was laughing about how idealistic we had been and how could we possibly have thought we could change a crop that was finished growing and ready to be harvested? Most of us don't want to look like fools and we rationalize what we hear, and then don't act on what we have heard, and that makes us fools in God's eye. Most of the time, when we pray to be used miraculously and then Father has the Spirit tell us to do something a bit out there or strange for us, (maybe unique would be better term to use), we instantly deny knowing whether it is God speaking to us or simply our desire. We know, but what we prayed for now appears a bit costly and could get us rejected or thought of as foolish. We need to recognize that many times rationalization could be, or is, the first step toward disobedience. It changes **God** to **good** and **good** has one too many "O's" in it, because good fits in with acceptance and acceptability. It changes what we heard into something more palatable and comfortable for us to do publicly, and then causes what we do to be without power, because it is a compromise. The Holy Spirit does not honor compromise of God's words or commands.

I am a man given to dreams and visions and in this walk I find that I cannot control either or cause them to come, but I have them fairly consistently. The reality of how God has always talked with men and communicated whom He is and what He wants to convey at any given time, seems to have not changed. Like scripture says, "There is no shadow of turning with the Lord and Jesus is the same yesterday, today and forever" (James and Hebrews). In the world and in many church meetings we are taught that voices, thoughts, visions and dreams should not be taken too seriously or trusted for guidance. In some aspects I say, "Yes" to this, but there is also something we must remember and not throw out. Nowhere in scripture does it say we should not trust Father or "know" the Voice of God. Even to come to Jesus and repent we must be "convicted by the Spirit" (Jn.16:8-13). John chapter 10 makes a strong statement about the fact that we should "know" His voice. Many other scriptures talk of people being spoken to by God or given visions and dreams that convey a message from Him to us. I am sure that others, like me, have had a lot of dreams, visions or other communications from the Lord that we have rebuked, believing that they were not God, only to find out later that they *were* God. Even after all these years of walking in His presence, and all my visions, dreams and encounters with the supernatural, I still have trouble accepting the fact that God talks to me. This is something that I find overwhelming, God talking to a speck of dust (me) on a speck of dust (the earth) in a universe that is probably a speck of dust in comparison to all that He has created.

In visions and dreams you see yourself doing or being a part of different scenarios. Many people fear sharing them because of the reproof from their peers or fear they will appear "super spiritual" or crazy. We have put such restrictions on the believer that most feel that they cannot share or ask to share a vision, dream or word from the Lord because they are not "mature or trained enough" to hear from God. This is a sad thing, as we have stopped a lot of what God would say to His church through our control or fear of embarrassment.

Most of our intimacy with God is lost through fears, intimidation, peer pressure, control and just plain bad teaching from past generations. Leaders are only doing what they knew, so there is no condemnation, but fear of new experiences have put some heavy restrictions on what they have passed to us. Scripture should not be something that controls us, but instead should be a liberating thing that brings people into intimate, dynamic fellowship and the presence of a mighty God. Whenever people have a freedom to live for the Audience of One, others will be brought into His Presence as they experience the same intimate fellowship with Him.

> Those who study a miracle Book without believing in miracles are doomed to deception.

The conclusion? I have had several tell me how to end this book of blunders and wonders. How do you end a story about a life lived with Jesus not over yet? I find myself looking ahead to more testimonies and stories to learn from and more life to live.

Several of my friends have encouraged me to end with an account of a visitation I had in 2007 in Indonesia. I awoke one morning to a room full of angels -- 13 of them to be exact. It was a very interesting experience of which I had never prayed for. I was not an "angel guy" nor am I after the encounter, but the experience was profound. In the bible it is never the angels that are important but the message they bring. It started in India a couple of months earlier on the same trip when I was told by Dr. Victor Chaudhrie, Randeep Matthews and another friend of mine there that I was in sin. The angels' visitation was at the end of a two and a half month time abroad. They repeated the declaration I had heard in India that morning in my room in Jakarta. As I awoke to find these angels in my room the first question came rushing out, "Why are you here?" The response from the one who appeared to be the spokesman was, "We are waiting for you." Another angel spoke with what I took as distain, "We are waiting for the church." At that moment the first angel spoke again, "You are in sin!" Another of the angels quipped, "The church is in sin." It was a flat type statement that he appeared to really dislike saying.

I knew what my sin was; not imparting to the body of Christ the intimacy I had discovered with Father, nor being able to give the

159

revelation of intimacy away like I should. (I need to live my life more fully with Father to have more of His presence and anointing to break the yokes that the church or the world is chained to). All of the miracles and salvations I have seen over the years are not enough. The angels were indeed telling me that, without speaking it specifically. I knew that I needed more of a relationship than I had and it would only come as I surrendered more to His love and presence.

I also knew the sin of the church; not living in the world in the intimate relationship with Father and Jesus that we are supposed to have, in such a way as to draw people to Father or to demonstrate that He is God! I also knew that leadership would be held accountable for not raising the church up into a place of close dynamic fellowship with Father, and for doing the "church's" ministry for the body.

There is much more to this revelation that came through the angels visit in my room and what has happened to me since, but let it suffice to say, our excuse of, "***We are waiting for God***" will not cut it anymore. He has done all He is going to do. **WE** need to move out and do what He has called us, commissioned us, and sent us to do – be a demonstration of "***knowing***" Jesus to the world, seeking and saving the lost and destroying the works of the enemy.

Two scriptures highlighted the encounter I had that morning, Matthew 7:21-27 and Luke 13:23-28. I will leave it to you to read them.

And one last thought, you remember the phone call I was waiting for? It came, only 17 ½ years after the vision, after I had given up on ever fulfilling what God had shown me. After I laid it down and said, "\Thanks for the journey of intimacy you have taken me on and

160

for the vision that compelled me forward to this relationship with Father and you, Jesus, I had found." The call came one month after that moment of surrendering the future I had lived for all these years. My dear friend George Hughes called me one morning and asked me, " Neil, would you like to go to India?" And now I am 11 years into the fulfillment of God's vision for my life and I am only 61!

Will write more later! neil